How to Draw Portraits

Jeremy Lee

Published by Guardian Cyber Tech. Book division., 2013.

While every precaution has been taken in the preparation of this book, the publisher assumes no responsibility for errors or omissions, or for damages resulting from the use of the information contained herein.

HOW TO DRAW PORTRAITS

First edition. March 14, 2013.

Copyright © 2013 Jeremy Lee.

ISBN: 979-8224511624

Written by Jeremy Lee.

Also by Jeremy Lee

How to Draw Portraits
It's About Time

Table of Contents

To my wife, family, and freinds.

Public Domain Source

The drawing on the cover of this book and also the same one shown within used a drawing reference from the public domain. It is entitled, "An Aymara woman praying in Bolivia" , where the original reference has been identified as being free of known restrictions under copyright law, including all related and neighboring rights.

About this book

After much practice, and interaction with other graphite artists, I've noticed that a specialised lexicon is common. These words and definitions are key to the ability to communicate process and technique to other artists. One of the barriers that I first encountered when seriously learning the craft was to find solid definitions of fundamental concepts as simple as the example 'value'. It is unfortunate that this word is in common use outside the disciplines of painting and illustration because that fact makes it difficult for the novice to isolate a relevant definition. In this book, we explore the language used by graphite artists in preparation for descriptions on how to produce effects like: 3D, pop, form, shadow, light, texture, weight, balance, pattern, layering, luminosity, contrast and so on. There are well over 100 illustrations to assist careful descriptions.

In art, detail is critical. I need to qualify this. Attention to detail comes from careful observation. This is an analytical process, which is a foundation of creativity. Only once you, as the creative entity, can appreciate the fine detail of what you depict, are you fully qualified to remove all that is not essential. The decision to remove or include detail depends on your artistic choices and reason for producing the artwork. Let's consider the following detailed visual statement about my left hand.

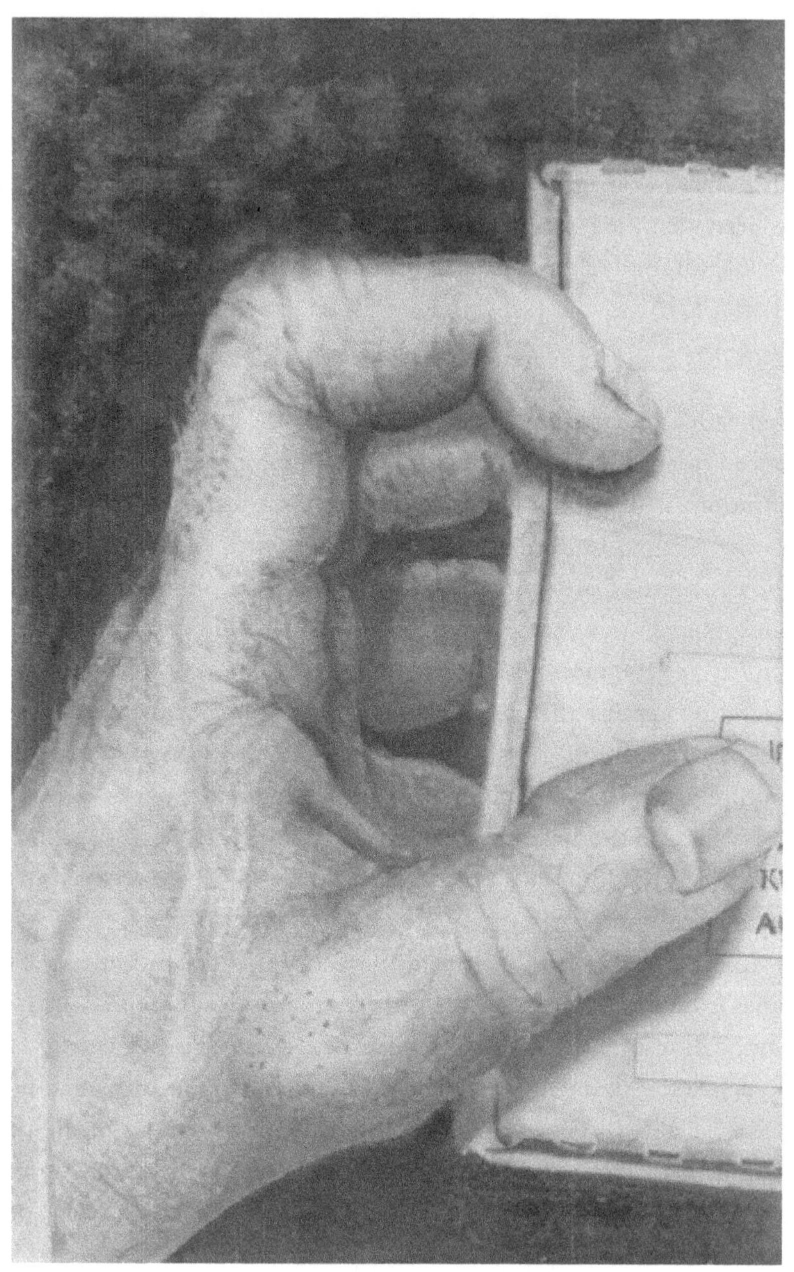

The first question about this work is, "What is it trying to say?" Only then can we decide what to leave out. The reason I drew this was as an exercise. It was to learn about skin texture, folds, tiny hairs, pores, shadow, form, value, tendons, bones, nails and so on. The idea is to communicate as many features about my hand as possible. To that end, no details once observed were to be left out. This extreme detail is at the other end of the scale when placed with works like that of Turner, Rothko, Mondrian and many others who sought to communicate with a very limited detail. There is no doubt in my mind that all these famous artists mastered the ability to observe fine detail.

Some might say, "The ideal level of detail is to remove everything that is not essential to the artwork." Such minimalist ideals have their place but like most idealistic philosophical goals, it can be limiting. For example, at what point do you stop removing detail? At what point does something that is easily described as art turn into nothing more than an object?

Don't forget that incredible detail fascinates the average observer so there is nothing wrong with expressing art in that way.

I am going to assume that you want to start from scratch. However, the techniques described in this book will also be useful to artists who are already skilled to use colour. This is because drawing is typically seen as a preparatory medium but when it is studied as a fine art, the new skills will get absorbed into the artist's existing techniques in other mediums. We will discuss the tools, media and techniques which are most basic for graphite drawing. A sketch is a preparatory task. A drawing is a finished piece; but a work of art is something much more. I intend to teach theory and technique slowly so you can work from basics to compose and execute a work of art after suitable practice.

There are many books which illustrate art and technique in various mediums, but few like this one which focus only on detailed and finished works in graphite and charcoal. You can also use many of the techniques presented here with chalk, coloured pencils and tinted paper but this book will only discuss graphite and charcoal on white paper.

Introduction

It's commonly taught that we either operate in a left-brain mode for logical mathematical and analytic thought, or a right-brain mode for creative and intuitive problem solving.

The left-brain, right-brain contest has, in my opinion, been overdone. We use all of our brain, all the time. Analytical processes and speech are processed in the left hemisphere; problem-solving logic is in the left hemisphere. Art—that is creative art as opposed to illustration or mechanical copying—is now almost universally called a right-brain activity. However, this is not the whole story.

We need to use both analytical and logical processes in tandem with non-verbal intuitive thought to be successfully creative, and to solve problems. One might be tempted to think that modern abstract art, and much contemporary art is purely a product of the right-brain. I challenge this. There are many poor abstract art creations in the market. It seems that anyone who can pick up a brush and slap some colours on to a canvas could be called an artist. There have been cases where the art critics have been totally fooled by these pieces of work, and I think that tells us more about the critics than the art. For example, take two-year-old Freddie W.R. Linsky, as chronicled in the UK's daily mail; armed with only pretentious and flowery words, his mother was able to convince a Manchester artist and collector to purchase Freddie's artwork. Even a gallery in Berlin wanted to showcase his 'talents'.

Excellent abstract art is invariably produced by people who are masters of drawing and technique. This is because good abstract art is hard. In a proper abstract work, all representational elements are removed, leaving other components of an artwork to do the work. These components must do more work than normal to be successful. One might be tempted to think that once the burden of representation is removed, there is little else to do but switch on that right brain and slap paint around. Nonsense—even in an abstract work, the artist cannot forget about balance, emotion, impact, dominant hue, complementary colours, weight, compositional elements, focal point, many other components of the painting, and light fastness, texture, translucency, permanence, drying rate, support-stability and myriad other left-brain knowledge. Similarly, just because the burden of hue has been removed, it does not trivialise the act of making good monochromatic art.

It is much harder to measure the success of an abstract work compared with a representational work. People are naturally more familiar with representational works, which makes it easier to judge.

I maintain that an artist must first be a technician to permit the creative process to succeed. To that end, this book is filled with a description of techniques. Visual mark-making artistic expression is not far removed from being a musician. The musician requires knowledge of notes, harmonies, layers, beat, riffs, melody and many deep technicalities on how to make a non-raucous noise from any particular instrument. Artists too, need to know how to make marks on paper using left-brain techniques. Artists who wish to make a lifelike representational work need to analyse the subjects deeply. This means that we need to look intently at objects. We must view them with a different goal than the non-artist. We need to consider how light strikes an object, how it is reflected, and where it goes after that. We need to know ways to simulate texture, form and value and look at negative space as well as the object itself. In a way, you need to teach your left-brain how and when to let go. If it makes sense to paint using your non-dominant hand, then this may well be a left-brain decision. Both hemispheres are necessary to produce art.

Once technique has become automatic, and you no longer need to work analytically, the creative process can come into play. What I hope to do in this book is to provide the tools to release creative freedom, and one of those tools, is to learn how to see like an artist. This means to abandon our normal way of looking, and submit to an observational view rather than a knowledge-based view that we so often use as non-artists. This also means being allowed to alter the representation of the subject under study for greater artistic effect, but only on the back of solid technique.

Definitions

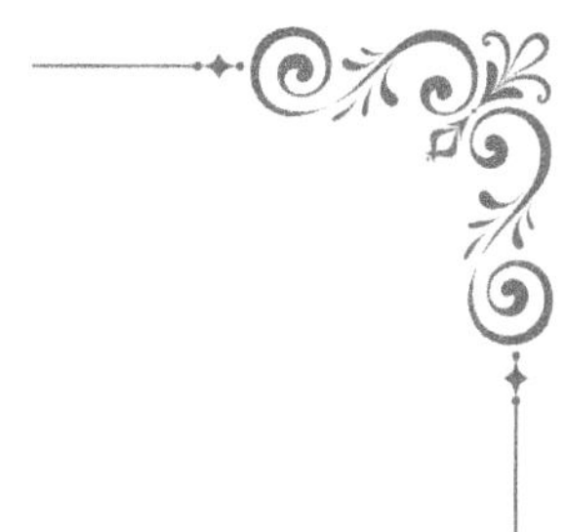

We will first define the language used in the rest of the book, as much as possible in the same way as specialist graphite artists do so from around the world. Once we have a language to use, it makes the tutorials and descriptions more precise and easier to follow. Please make sure you understand the terms used because efficient communication depends on agreed semantics.

The old masters often used charcoal as a preparatory medium. These works were not intended to last long. Charcoal is charred wood, so it was cheap. It is still cheap, and it produces wonderful deep darks without shine; but it smudges easily. It was also used to sketch on a canvas then obscured with the painting layers. Today a plastic (acrylic) is available in a spray called fixative. This fixative is supplied by art-shops in a spray can. Fixative may be used over charcoal or graphite to make it stick harder to the paper and reduce the chance of smudging. You may also frame your works behind glass. Today, there is a slow but growing interest in finished graphite and charcoal works. You will still find however, that colour paintings are very popular. Colour helps to finish the decor in a room where the rest of the furnishings and walls are neutral colours. Where you find impressive colour already on the walls, black-and-white drawings and photographs have pleasing impact. If there is a trend towards more colourful walls in homes and offices, graphite works will be more marketable than they have been in the latter part of the 20th century.

Time

Be prepared to alter your sense of time for this kind of work.

A sketch is a quick outline or shading which takes only minutes or at most a few hours. When you start to add fine detail and layer upon layer as represented in this book, the time to complete a rendering will be significant. It can take anywhere from six to five hundred hours to complete a work, depending of course on the size, detail, and technique. You will need to prepare your mind to tackle something so significant. Even if you work a full-time job unrelated to art, here are some thoughts which will help you.

• Most people in western culture spend about 4 hours a day watching TV. That's around 1,460 hours in a year. In one year, you could produce 36 drawings each taking 40 hours to complete by not watching TV. Or produce about ten drawings by dedicating one hour a day to your craft. There may be as much as 20 minutes of ads on TV each hour, so it's possible to progress well with a drawing just by working on it while the ads play.

• If you take the train to work, it is smooth enough to complete some of the less detailed areas. This makes good use of otherwise dead time.

• Half an hour before starting work in a coffee shop gives you quiet time to draw. It also calms the mind and helps you to prepare for the rest of the day.

• Lunchtime might be a sociable activity for you at work, but sometimes instead, drawing will split the day and reduce stress.

• Ask yourself whether you would like to produce 300 sketches or four amazing works of art and a significant number of sketches in one year.

Once you commit to a work, don't stress about how long it will take. There is no need to rush.

If you decide to make a living from producing and selling art, there are three options. One might spend a long time producing an original and sell it for many thousands, or make prints and sell many copies. Or one might produce many cheap uninspiring works and sell them at a reasonable cost so people in the street can buy an original artwork and feel proud to have a unique work on the wall. Of course, the dream might be to paint quickly and sell for a fortune, but that depends on becoming famous—being famous is likely to be more dependent on good marketing than good art.

That last observation is not to suggest you should produce low quality art—it is to emphasise that marketing your work is an important commercial endeavour. With good marketing, and great art, your chances of making a living at your craft are greater than simply making a good product.

The particular techniques taught in this book consume a lot of time, but you might produce a body of work that will, one day hang in a museum. Your work will be passed down to your children and grandchildren. A detailed realistic portrait of a relative will hold strong interest to your family forever.

Our Language

As with any specialty, a long list of jargon develops. It is appropriate to dedicate a section to describe the words that we use to make the rest of the book more easily understood. There are two ways that I could approach this. The first is as it comes. The second is alphabetical order. I think the former is more attractive and useful because we can uncover the terms as they are about to be put into context.

Technique

Throughout this book, I have frequently and necessarily used the word, "technique". Technique is a mechanical operation applied as a process to produce a predictable result. At first, this seems in opposition to the embodiment of what is art because art is about creativity, which is supposed to be free and novel without a care for procedure and rules. If that were true, you would not need technique in the same way that an architect would not need his load-tables, or a hairdresser would not need to know how to layer hair, and a potter would not need to make a round pot. Technique is the foundation of art, and I think creativity is an illusion cast over technique to push it into apparent insignificance. Without technique, you cannot create. Unfortunately, you can develop technique and never be creative. These so-called rules and procedures are therefore, constantly under question. Feel free to break those rules—bend those rules, and modify those rules—but do so in the full knowledge of what you change.

Realism

Realism refers to artwork which attempts to depict something recognisable. In the extreme, it attempts to do this with great accuracy so the viewer is at awe with the likeness of the subject. An abstract work on the other hand attempts to remove all recognisable objects from the picture. Somewhere on a sliding scale between abstract and extreme realism lies impressionism.

The aim of the techniques in this book is to produce works which are almost photographic. Photorealistic works attempt to fool the viewer into thinking they are looking at a photograph.

A photograph has limitations like a compressed depth of field and limited tonal range. It may also have problems or characteristics which alter perspective. A photorealistic work often attempts to duplicate these limitations. Our work aims to duplicate the detail of a photograph or exceed it. We reserve the right to introduce a different or more extended tonal range, and better contrast and focus. In fact, as a graphite portrait artist, we have none of the limitations enforced on a photographer.

There is no reason we cannot draw something that is impossible to construct or observe in nature. We will try to produce works that are realistic, might look at first sight like a photocopy or photograph, but closer inspection will reveal pencil marks and hints that make the work recognisable as a drawing. One of the strongest criticisms of photorealistic work is to question whether it adds anything more than simply taking a photo. This seems, at least at a superficial level to be a valid concern, so let's progress with an underlying freedom of expression away from purely photographic-style reproduction.

Impressionism

An impressionistic artwork uses a minimum of individually recognisable shapes, shades and colours, but somehow conveys the whole artwork as a depiction of something real. As you look at an impressionistic artwork up-close, it is like an abstract, but as you stand away from it, optical colour mixing, or optical blending of tones force the viewer to hover on the brink of a representational experience.

Depth of field

This refers to how much is in focus. When you take a picture, the right amount of light is required on the photographic film. Too much light will cause the picture to be washed out, and too little light causes it to be too dark. Traditional photographic film is more or less sensitive to light depending on its chemical composition. You can get fast films, which are sensitive to light, and slow films, which require more light.

Depending on available light when you take the picture, you need to control how much reaches the film. There are two ways to control how much light lands on the film. The first is to control how long the shutter remains open. The second is to control the size of the shutter hole. The size of the shutter hole is called the aperture. A big aperture lets more light in for a given shutter speed. A small aperture obviously does the opposite. It is important to understand that a small aperture causes light to hit the film near a 90 degree angle. Where these light beams cross will give good focus, and for a small aperture, there is considerable slackness in how we focus the lens onto the film. Alternatively, you can consider that a range from near objects to far objects will be in good focus for a small aperture. But as the aperture is opened wider, light can strike the film at a more obtuse angle and the range at which all these light beams cross is narrowed. This means less depth in your subject is in good focus. If you have more light, or a faster film, you can get away with a smaller aperture, and get more of the picture in focus. But this effect is controlled by physics, and the photographer must work with the limitations. The same argument holds for digital cameras except instead of a film, there is a light-sensitive electronic sensor known as a charge-coupled-device (CCD).

To put this into practice, let's imagine that we are taking a picture of someone's face. Imagine that you focus the camera on the person's nose, and there is little light, and you are using a slow-speed film. You will need a wide aperture, which means only the tip of the person's nose will be in focus. This is a shallow depth of field. With a subject that does not move, we could take several pictures at different focal points, and stitch them together using a computer to create a single low-light image with a good depth of field. If we are drawing a person from life, we can do this on paper without technical limitations. We focus only on one part of the face at a time, and can draw each part in focus as required. Despite this, the public are familiar with photographs, and you may wish to emulate this limited depth of field to create impact.

When a portion of your drawing is in focus compared with another part, it will stand out. We can use this as part of our composition. By defocusing confusing details, like images in the background, we can create more interest in the subject matter. The defocused images can be thought of as a kind of impressionism.

Blur

When you take a photograph, or glimpse a fast-moving object, its outlines seem to be smeared in the direction of travel. This is obvious in a photograph of a moving object if the shutter speed is slow compared with the speed of the object. In a drawing, we can create a feeling of movement by smearing the outlines of suitable objects. You have to be careful though. It is possible to over-use a technique like this and create a visual cliché.

Visual cliché

A cliché is normally associated with a verbal statement which has been over-used, like:

- Not my cup of tea.
- Everything happens for a reason.
- No love lost.
- Absolutely.
- You can't have your cake and eat it too.
- Simple as pie.

Clichés are usually to be avoided. (It's tempting to say "like the plague" but that's been done before [time and time again].)

In visual arts, we also have clichés. Some examples are:

- An advert for a product features a very good-looking customer.
- Widely used standard clip-art in presentations.
- An ostrich with its head in the ground.
- Frying an egg on the pavement, car or bald-head.
- A cartoon character whose legs look like a spinning windmill.
- A financial-chart with an upward or downward pointing arrow.

You will find many visual clichés in the art and advertising world. They are boring and unimaginative. Your challenge as a developing artist is to describe and deliver your message with impact and do so in new and exciting ways. This usually means avoiding the visual cliché. It's more difficult than you imagine. Galleries actively avoid cliché work. Instead, they look for originality.

Impact

Impact is associated with a sudden change and exchange of energy. When a hammer hits a chunk of metal, we can imagine the impact. This concept of a sudden and forceful change of energy is used as an analogy in multiple ways. We talk of the impact of waste on the environment or an impact-statement in business. It's associated with a disturbance, and in general, a "wow factor". For a drawing to have impact, we want it to make people stop and think. It might be shocking or high contrast or jagged. There are no rules for creating impact, but you will know it when you see it. Impact can be sudden or subtle as it might be hidden in the meaning of a work, such that the impact remains dormant until the viewer suddenly sees something new. An example might be a composition of a group of people chatting. They might at first be seen as casually talking, but as the viewer lingers on the content, he or she may suddenly realise they are about to be given some terrible news. The impact might be delivered by characters in the background who may be out of focus. Impact, therefore is any element of the work where a sudden exchange of information bursts into the mind of the viewer.

Impact is often obvious—as in an example where strong, detailed, high-contrast diagonal lines force the viewer's eye to the main subject matter. If you want to convey peace and tranquillity, high-impact tricks might not be useful. You need to use it in the right context, and in the right amount.

Grain

Ideally, each point which is recorded on a photographic film is tiny. It's usually so small that you cannot see it as a single grain but as the film speed rises, the grains get bigger. When large enough, the grain is clearly visible. When a photograph is taken in low light, a fast film is required, and fine details are sacrificed. In technically ideal terms, grain is undesirable but in a work of art, whether this is photography or hand drawn, you can use grain to convey a message. A grainy image might be a smaller part of a composition. The grainy image could also be the main subject matter. An image which conveys a smoky subdued or mysterious atmosphere might benefit from a grainy texture. You can use a grainy rendering near the focal point to help enhance the composition.

When drawing, you can either draw grain on smooth paper, or you can use rough paper so the texture of the paper provides the grainy appearance. A technique called pointillism could be thought of as exploiting grain. Using little dots rather than lines is a way to induce optical-mixing in the mind of the viewer. Sometimes, this is very effective as it causes a luminous effect. It was a popular-science-writer by the name of Michel Eugène Chevreul who made the scientific research of Helmholtz and Newton's colour system understandable. Art historians credit Georges Pierre Surat for first using this technique.

Tonal range

In music, tone refers to a characteristic shape of the notes which make up the music so two notes of the same fundamental frequency sound different—because they have different harmonics. In drawing, tone is the level of intensity of a mark on the page with reference to how much light it reflects. This is also called value. Tonal range is a way to talk about the difference between the darkest dark, and the lightest light.

A good tonal range is necessary for high contrast. The number of distinct steps between the darkest dark and the lightest light in the range will control the smoothness, detail, and general feel of the drawing. In the same way as a simple piece of music might only have a few notes, a drawing might only have a few tones.

In the value scale below you see black, white, and a continuous transition between the two. For realistic drawing, this is the kind result you should aim for.

Another way to view this is on a histogram. Many computer-based packages provide a feature that shows the histogram, and you can use it to gauge the range of values in your drawing. Scan the drawing into your computer, and find the histogram.

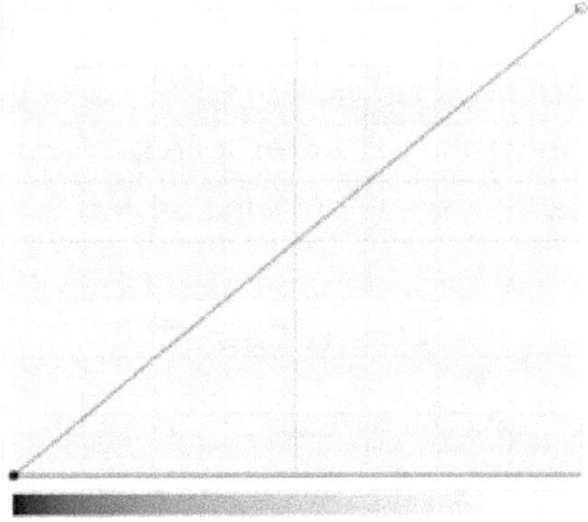

Below this histogram, you can see a value. The vertical scale and light grey bar chart shows how much of each value is present in the picture. This particular histogram is from the computer-generated value scale shown above and therefore it is near to ideal. Your actual pictures will not look like this. It will not be possible to get the blackest or whitest extremes for a typical drawing.

The next example is one of the author's high-contrast drawings. Note how the histogram is bunched to the left. Despite this, the range of values extends far to the right which is because the woman's face is considerably lighter than the background.

The dark values were made with a carbon pencil. There are no perfectly white values because the whitest you can get is that of the paper and no paper is perfectly white. Because of this, your main goal for creating high impact realistic drawings is to develop your skills to create dark values on bright white paper.

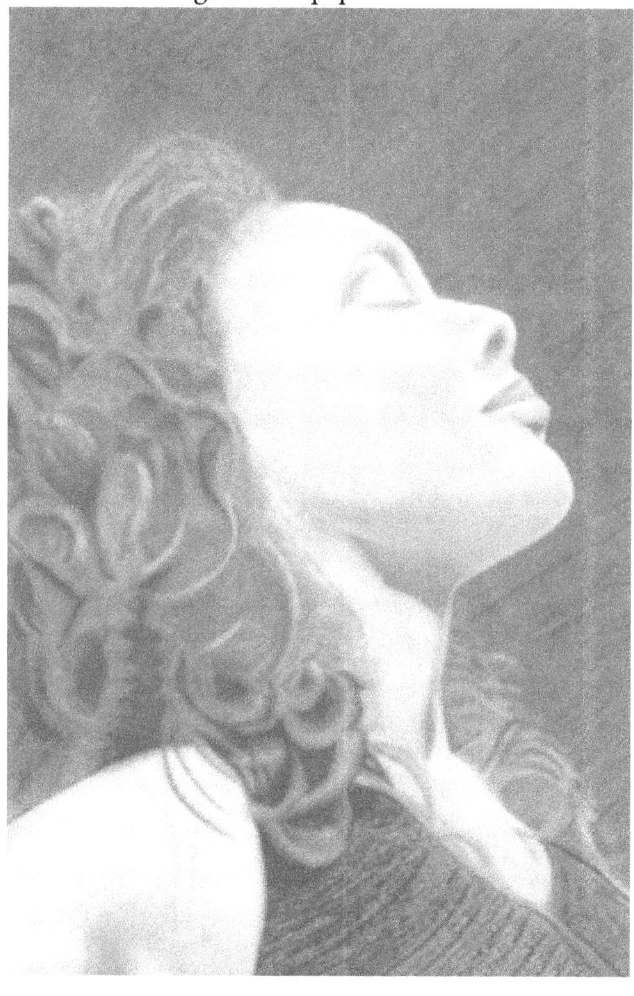

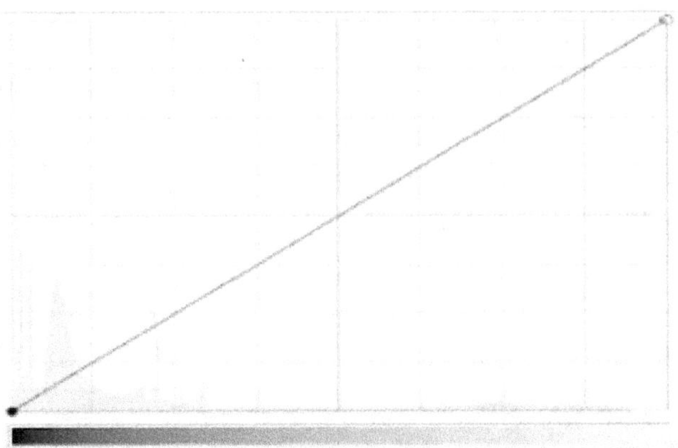

Next is the histogram of a nice drawing found on the internet (not shown here)

but although it's well drawn, it lacks impact. It's a typical pencil drawing with poor dark values.

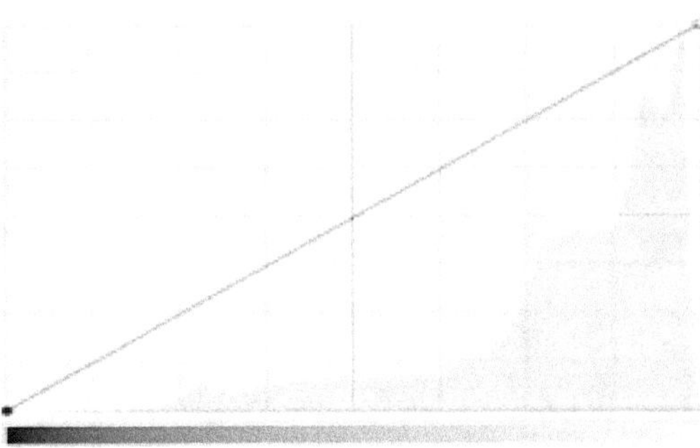

The whole histogram is bunched up to the right and contains a high percentage of bright values. Try instead to aim for a balanced range of tones.

If there are only two or three values, and the range is high, it makes a poster-like picture with high contrast. If these tones are close in value, the tonal range is compressed. Detailed drawings will benefit from a high number of tonal values, but you can still produce fine detail with few values. For example, detailed pen-and-ink drawings only use two values—black ink on white paper.

Your choice of tonal range and number of steps affects the mood of your art. We might refer to compressing or expanding the tonal range as appropriate. For the smoky nightclub scene mentioned earlier, use a compressed tonal range. For a dramatic moody portrait a wide tonal range might work well. Note: dynamic range is usually used to describe the ability of a medium to represent dark to light values; while tonal range is an artistic choice.

The way that you gradually take a dark area to a light area is called a transition. (See also sfumato). If you use pointillism, different values are simulated by controlling the density and size of the dots. Note: You can use pointillism on top of continuous-valued techniques.

Midtones

The midtone is a value which is approximately half way between the darkest dark and general highlights. If a portrait has typical lighting, the midtones will make up a large part of the skin. Hair and clothing could go either way depending on the colour and lighting. It is important to find and maintain good midtones. It is also important to move from one tone to another in a smooth transition as dictated by the underlying form. By example, an egg is a smooth form, and so the transitions from light to dark also need to be smooth, but a cube has edges. The cube's edges must also be rendered with a realistically smooth transition, but the rate of this transition is rapid. Along the faces of the cube, a subtle transition is often seen and this transition usually flows through close values smoothly. When you add texture to a surface, this is to alter the smoothness of the transitions at the small-scale, while preserving overall transitions for the gross form. Midtones are particularly sensitive when depicting tone and texture.

Value (tones)

For many, if not most graphite portraits, it is important to establish the blackest black that you can get and use it in the deepest shadows. The whiteness of the paper is naturally the other end of the tonal range.

We talked about value in the section on tonal range. Strictly, value is a measure of how much light is reflected off the surface. Different colours will have varying reflectivity (value), so a light-green and a certain yellow might be at the same value even though they are different colours. In black-and-white images, value is independent of colour since there is only really one colour (grey). If you were to make a black-and-white drawing of a bowl of fruit, you would need to make a judgement on the relative values of the orange and banana. Some parts of the banana will have a darker value than some parts of the orange, and vice versa, but overall you would expect the orange to be a darker value than the banana if it is viewed in the same light.

Things in a shadow naturally have darker values. Often, I use the term tone and value interchangeably. However, different mediums, that is graphite, carbon and charcoal, have a slightly different colour in which case the word "tone" is apt. Charcoal against Carbon looks soft and only when juxtaposed will you see they also have a slightly different hue, so it's tempting to use "tone" to mean something a little more than simple value. Most of the art industry uses the word value.

Simultaneous contrast

When a very dark value is placed next to a very light value, the light one will look white. When that same light value is surrounded by a value only slightly deeper, it will look grey. Your choice of background and depth of shadows will affect the value-range of the midtones.

The nasolabial furrow is a crease extending from the side of the nose to the ends of the mouth. The philtrum is a vertical depression in the centre of the upper lip, directly under the tip of the nose. Both cast shadows. Both are surrounded normally by bright areas, and therefore appear darker than they really are. Beginners might draw these too dark because they are unaware of simultaneous contrast.

It's a good idea to apply the darkest values as soon as you are happy with the overall composition and proportions. Don't do it before you are confident because dark values are hard to remove.

Perception and seeing are different. Simply seeing something is describable in a mechanical way. However perception involves the brain and the mechanical process of seeing.

There is a famous illustration by Edward H. Adelson, Copyright 1995, that shows this effect to an extreme. In that illustration, there is a light green solid cylinder casting a shadow over a chequerboard. There are two identical values, one in the shadow, and one outside but it is impossible to judge correctly without masking them off. The effect is not subtle; it is profound and very difficult to believe what you perceive. However, squinting at it gives some strong clues because it mutes out surrounding distractions and allows you to see absolute value more accurately.

This illusion is available at

<u>https://en.wikipedia.org/wiki/Checker_shadow_illusion</u>[1]

---

1. https://en.wikipedia.org/wiki/Checker_shadow_illusion

Shading

Look around at the objects you see. Every surface is not uniform in value even if it is physically flat. As light falls on an object, it is reflected at an angle. Light does not fall evenly across the surface, and objects nearby alter the values in the surface. For a curved surface, the level of light reaching your eye depends mostly on your current viewpoint. Therefore, a curved surface will have a high number of values. The way that you draw the transition between two given values is called shading or rendering. Almost no objects have distinct lines.

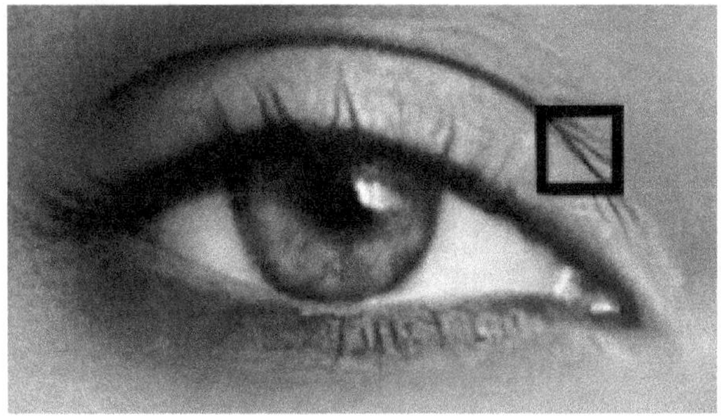

Here is a picture of an eye. Look closely at the "line" that forms the crease in the eyelid.

Most objects are best represented by a continuous gradation between light and dark. If you look at a person's face, there are no hard lines.

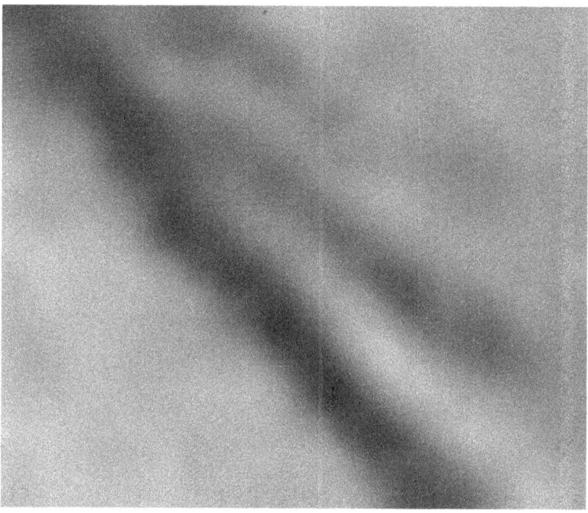

You might at first perceive a wrinkle as a line, but a closer look will show a gradual change in value from light to dark to light to dark again. For realistic work, try to use shading however, for a cartoon-like effect or something else that you have in mind or feel like experimenting with, try using hard lines.

Note how this is an abstract shape. There are no actual lines—only gradual movement from shadow to light and back. This keen observation is most important for realistic drawing.

Please note, there are no rules here, only guidelines, and in no way do I wish to restrict your artistic expression. If you find a way to use hard lines to good effect, then use them. One of the most impressive line drawings I have seen was a contour drawing of Lawrence of Arabia. It was constructed with hard lines in pen-and-ink. The drawing was minimal and it would be degraded by the removal of any single line. But that drawing, good as it is, is not a realistic graphite representation which is the subject of this particular book.

Shadow

The part of an object which has almost no light is in a shadow. Details are muted or lost, limiting the tonal range. When detail is present in a shadow, it is caused by reflected light and this guarantees weaker illumination. You can exploit this fact by paying close attention to removing unwanted highlights in a shadowed part of your drawing. Limit the value-range in the depths of a shadow.

One of the challenges with a pencil rendering is to prevent the pencil marks from shining. Try filling an area of white paper with a soft pencil by pressing hard. Hold it at an angle, and it will reflect light. You don't want this. The techniques in this book describe ways to prevent or minimise this. Completely filling the paper's tooth is another challenge; if you draw a shaded area and leave some of the white paper showing, it will not look like a real shadow.

Despite a limited value-range in shadows, you still find transitions. Photographic references often lose them, and if you simply copy a photograph, then—unsurprisingly—the resulting artwork looks typically like it was copied from a photograph. Critics, art-lovers and collectors are likely to pass it by. Discover what is in the shadows, and introduce this into your artwork. A good way to do this is to keenly observe real-life subjects and use your imagination. A better way is to draw from life, but that is not often practical and is sometimes impossible, as with a posthumous portrait. Often, if the image is in a digital form, you can play with the parameters to peer deep inside the shadows—just to find out what would be seen with the live subject. To do this, look for an option called "curves" in your photo-editing software, and use it to temporarily brighten the darker values.

Highlights

If you are drawing on white paper, the brightest highlight will be the paper itself. Most paper is slightly cream coloured, so it's a good idea to find paper which suits your needs. Once you lay down graphite onto the paper, it is difficult to remove all of it. This means that you need to plan your brightest highlights and avoid drawing in that space until the last moment. Except for a bright point that you might find on the corner of a shiny object, or the highlight in a wet object, a highlight should not be completely white. Even then, the edges of the highlight are likely to be smeared rather than a definite line. Where needed, you can use an eraser to lift graphite from the paper to create slightly subdued highlights. We will talk more about this drawing method.

Drawing

You can draw with a pencil, a pen, a stick of chalk or a piece of burnt wood, or with paint! It's not the medium which defines drawing—but more the way marks are made on the paper. Drawing can be done in full colour too, so it's not just for monochrome work. You can also make an abstract drawing so it is not confined to the subject matter. The term seems to be hard to define; yet we know the difference between a sketch, a drawing and a painting when we see it. A drawing looks precise and has detail. The marks made on the paper are controlled and the result has a defined feel to it. Some art critics might complain about a painting if it looks drawn rather than painted, yet there exist some exquisite paintings that are, technically, drawings. Again, this illustrates the latitude one has in art when considering so-called rules.

Rendering

Rendering is the process of filling in a shape with correct shading and creating the impression of texture and form. During rendering, carefully reproduce the way light and shade play on the subject. Most of the content of this book is concerned with rendering. We need to learn how to duplicate shape and contour, but rendering will take the most time and the most practice.

Shape

Shape is easy to define. A circle is round, a playing card is flat and square, and a random doodle has a more complex curved shape. In particular, shapes make up bigger pictures. One of the ideas that we will explore is how small abstract shapes, when fitted together, will produce a realistic whole. Much of our process will be to identify abstract shapes in the subject matter, and duplicate those in our drawing. When defining individual shapes, learn how to disconnect these shapes from the surrounding context. Our mind makes us draw the wrong thing if we are too aware of the overall picture. The best way to illustrate this is to find a large poster-photo, then mask off all but a 1cm square. You will probably not be able to find a line or a recognisable object by looking only at 1cm at a time. You will, however, see abstract shapes and smooth gradations from light to dark. The trained artist will see these shapes without the aid of a mask. The grid method of transfer is good training for reproducing abstract shapes.

Form

Shape is a two-dimensional (2D) notion. Form is the 3D equivalent. When light plays on a two-dimensional object, the reflected light is a simple gradation in tone or a simple flat tone throughout. But a 3D object reflects incident light through many angles. Your viewpoint only collects the rays of light from one angle. This means that to represent form, you need to vary the tonal transitions accordingly. To do this, think about where the light comes from, the angle that it hits the object, and the angle that it leaves the object. Remember the ray of light will leave the object at the same angle that it hit. This is most obvious for a shiny surface. On a rough surface the texture causes fewer rays to reflect exactly to your viewpoint because the rough surface scatters the light in more directions. Consequently, smooth shiny surfaces have sharp well-defined transitions, while rougher surfaces have less defined transitions.

4D

Your paper is two-dimensional (2D). It might seem a little silly to try to make a four-dimensional (4D) representation on a two-dimensional surface. But let's think about this. We are happy to depict a 3D object on the 2D surface of the paper, so there should be no fundamental reason why we cannot depict a 4D scene on paper. The fourth dimension I am thinking of is that of time. When we take a photograph, it freezes a tiny slice of time and compresses it onto a two-dimensional surface. This can give stunning and dramatic effects but it has limitations. An object in motion will move during this tiny time-slice, and this will cause motion blur. A good photographer can take advantage of this by either panning the object to displace motion blur onto the background, or keep the background fixed and let the moving subject blur.

The fourth dimension—depicted with motion blur.

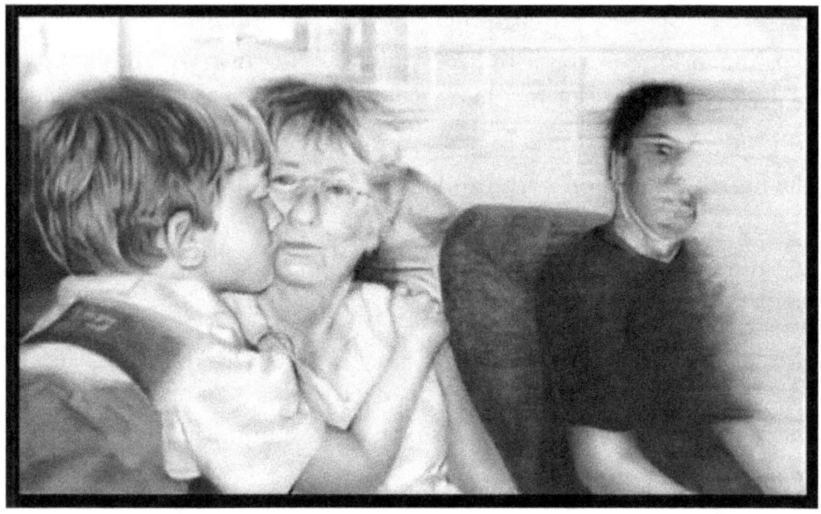

In this scene, we can see time. The young boy kisses his Mum tenderly, she responds, but his bigger brother anticipated this and reeled in mock disgust. You can see the sequence, even though the picture is laid out in only two dimensions. The relative motion blur aids this as the older boy has moved into the light in the background which obscures part of his face.

The results of course are difficult to control. However, when it is successful, it will give you a sense of time.

Motion blur is not the only way to represent time on a 2D surface. As an artist, you have no technical limitations of the camera. You can choose to draw or paint things in ways that are impossible to photograph. You can depict hidden surfaces which might suggest what is about to be revealed to a person viewing the scene. You can depict movement and anticipation. Incidentally, movement can also be an important part of an abstract piece. It's harder to describe than movement in a realistic object, but, movement can be suggested with non-realistic shape and form. You can depict history though careful composition. For example, objects which have just hit the floor will appear broken, and the expression on a person's face could combine with this to suggest what has just happened. It is difficult to describe this 4D effect, but to know that it is "out there" is a great advantage. The next time you go to an art viewing, ask yourself, "Why does this painting seem static, and why does that painting seem alive?" The chances are the livelier painting has somehow integrated the fourth dimension. It could be an expression on a person's face, or the configuration of objects in the air. It might be through the play of light and focus.

Light

Obviously, without light, you can't see. Light which reaches your eyes causes your mind to see the object. But from an artistic sense, there is more to it than this simplistic statement of physics. When a painting has light, it glows and lives.

There must be millions of good drawings and paintings which don't make the best use of light, and therefore remain only good pieces of art rather than great pieces of art.

Often, in western society and those that read left to right, the observer will also "read" a painting or drawing from left to right. Therefore, it is common to find the light coming from the top-left. However, such "rules" should be flexible, and some dramatic effects can be had by using two or more sources of light, and lighting the subject from below or directly from one side. Whatever you choose to do, try to make *light* work for you.

Negative space

Beginners often draw the shapes and objects which concentrate on the subject. This might be an apple, pear, banana and a bowl. If, however, you consider relative position of items, and instead, draw the shapes which make up the space between the objects, then you get a different understanding of what you are seeing. These negative spaces are part of the composition. Sometimes, a negative space is more important than the objects, and it will often contribute to the overall result of your drawing in an unconscious but significant way. When you draw negative space, you use the more "arty" sections of your brain because these shapes are usually abstract. Since they are abstract, you can draw what you see, and not what your logical part of your brain tells you to see.

Whether you use a photographic or live reference, it's common to draw what you know and not what you see. Initially, this often leads to an average or poor result. The problem stems from how our brain works. We symbolise features, so an eye and a mouth get abstracted to a standard simplified shape. It is as though our brains store a set of approximations and they work like pattern-matching machines.

It's likely the non-artist looks at a person's features briefly while the seasoned artist will focus on a particular area or shape and study it deeply. As you do more drawing, you will find that your interest lays not so much in the symbol of a mouth or nose, but in the way shadows fall over contours, and how light reveals imperfections in skin.

Study of negative space aids this artistic way of viewing the world. In some complex scenes, where the foreground consists of many tiny shapes—like tree-branches or hair—it is often easier to draw negative spaces before filling in foreground-detail.

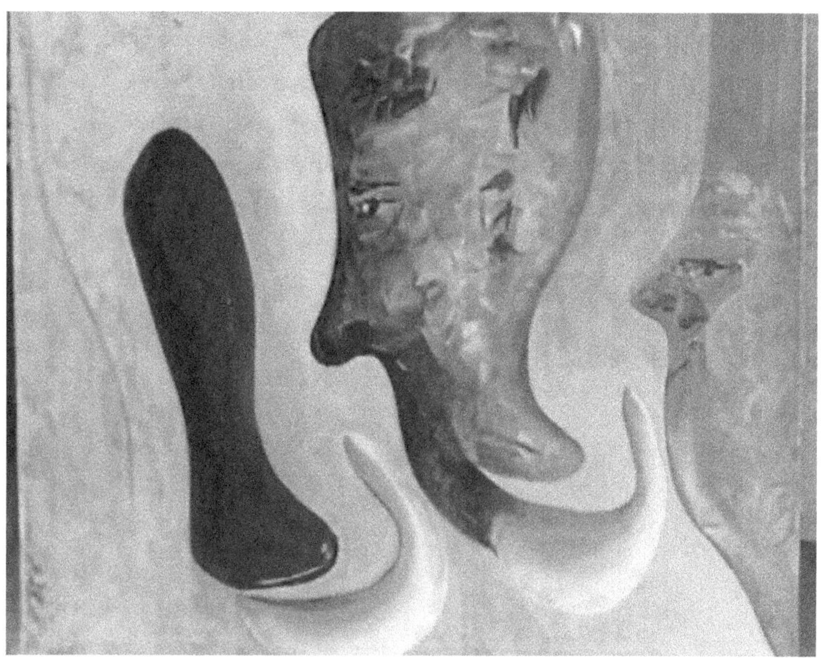

The illustration above is a grey-scale photograph of a full colour painting by the author. It tricks the viewer by forcing negative shapes into prominence while relegating the actual subject into a state where they are not immediately seen (stylised stiletto shoes). This effect is more pronounced in the full colour version because the colours help to make the illusion. Additionally, the negative spaces exploit how the human mind likes to see faces where faces are not strongly depicted. Finally, the negative spaces have distinct form.

Contour

Contour is an outline. Usually, there is contrast between a subject and the background. This contrast might be with colour, value, focus, texture or a combination. The contour of the object is a line which follows the boundary. You can make a contour drawing which will successfully represent an object even if the proportions are poor, and the shading and texture is absent.

The illustration below depicts essential contours with short, independent straight lines. Alternatively, you can try an exercise to draw a single smooth contour without either looking at the paper, or lifting the pencil. In this case, you stare at the subject, and concentrate only on the contour. Proportion and shape is not important to the exercise.

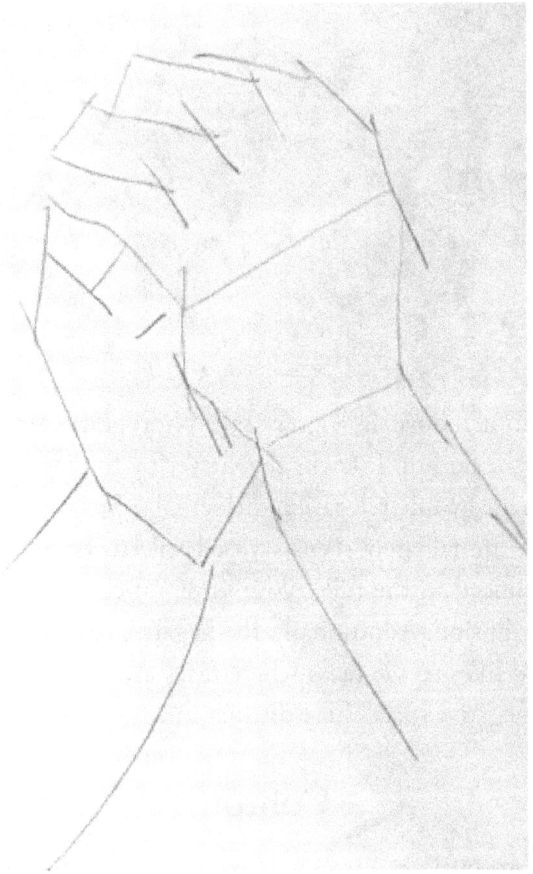

In this rough contour drawing, the outline of the subject is all that is drawn. It is not even drawn carefully or with any detail. The simple lines just indicate where the boundaries are.

When we draw a portrait, a preliminary contour drawing is useful. If our preliminary contour drawing is proportionally accurate, we may wish to extend the concept inside our object to identify abstract shapes within. This will aid us in the rendering stage. It's advisable to make the contour lines faint and use a soft pencil. Usually, the contour lines will be erased or covered during rendering.

Sketch

A sketch is a quick drawing. Sketches are useful tools to explore shape, value, contrast, texture and composition. It will be useful to create many rapid sketches of parts and the whole before finally committing to a full rendering. You might sketch someone's ear twenty times from different angles just to get a good feel for the final picture. When you do this, it makes the final rendering easy.

Weight

There are two kinds of weight relevant to our drawing. One is a measure of how heavy is the paper. This is measured in gsm (grams per square meter). The weight of paper is measured by the physical weight of 500 full-size sheets. It is given in grams or pounds. A typical useful weight for drawing is 220 gsm. Heavier papers will cost more and are likely to cope with rough-handling. Light paper will crease easily, and it will not be easy to use an eraser without damaging it.

Another kind of weight is about composition. If you draw a cone standing on its point, this cone—even though it is just on a piece of paper—is compositionally weighted at the top and it feels unstable.

We expect objects to look heavier at the bottom. When you frame a picture, it is conventional to put a mat around the picture, and that mat sits in the frame. The border of this frame is often made wider at the bottom to add visual weight. This helps the picture to sit on something substantial.

To add weight, we might add more detail in the foreground, greater contrast, and an overall darker tone to the lower foreground.

Scumble

For oil and acrylic painting, scumbling is a technique to drag a lighter colour over a darker one, where the lighter colour is more opaque. The overall effect is as if a transparent layer has been applied on top.

A realistic shadow should be thin, insubstantial, free of significant reflections and bear nothing in particular for your eye to rest upon. By this, I mean that you are unlikely to find highlights in a shadow area.

Many beginners draw shadow areas and still permit the white of the paper to show through. This is because it's harder to make the graphite penetrate.

The midtones and highlights are opposite to this. Highlights should be opaque and solid.

In a painting, scumbling is used to link midtones to highlights. A 3D effect is enhanced by keeping highlights opaque and things that recede transparent.

Usually, the transition from mid values to shadow is around a plane where the light no longer reflects directly into your eye from the viewing point. Therefore, this transition is receding and benefits from a degree of transparency.

Obviously, scumbling has a more limited meaning for a graphite drawing but we can exploit the same idea in the following way: Shadows in your drawing should saturate the paper so little or no tooth shows, and the tone will be compressed and dark compared with the midvalues—just as a shadow should be. The mid values will probably consist of harder graphite, more defined pencil marks, and texture where the texture is deliberately drawn or inherited from the paper's tooth. For a graphite drawing, you can use a scumbling technique to join these two areas. Try honing a wooden pencil to a cone-shape and use the flat of the cone to bring the darks into the lights. To do this, hold the pencil at a shallow angle so it has maximum contact, and gently drag it from dark to light. You can adjust this effect by using various grades of pencil with a smooth wedge shape to introduce the shadowed area into the highlight. It is important to increase tone and detail gradually as the transition goes from dark to light. By holding the pencil this way, graphite is deposited on the tips of the paper's tooth to leave other details showing through from the layer below. Although the shadows have a compressed range of values, they should still contain muted detail. Flat shadows limit the potential liveliness of an artwork.

Balance

Related to weight, is balance. The left-right composition of a work should usually have similar weight. If you ignore this, the composition might feel somehow uncomfortable. Bear in mind there are several ways to create weight, and the two sides of the drawing don't need to use the same technique for good balance. You could use contrast on one side, and focus on the other. It should be an intuitive thing: try it, see if it has a good feeling, adjust, experiment, and finally settle on something. As with any rule in art, bend it or break it as necessary to make a strong statement. You might deliberately cause imbalance for a dramatic effect, to control the composition or for some other reason. A classic example of an unbalanced composition is one where a picture of an adult elephant is on one side, and the baby on the other. I remember a cartoon where two dumb burglars are carrying that picture out, and one of them complains that he got the heavy end.

Tooth

If paper were very smooth, you would not be able to draw on it. The roughness of paper is called tooth. Very rough paper resists fine detail but is easy to draw on. The grade of pencil that you choose will make a different mark on smooth paper compared with rough paper. This is because the size of the tooth works differently with the hardness and softness of various lead-types.

Pencil lead is not really lead. It is made from a composition of graphite and clay. After a while you will notice that different papers display a line from any given pencil with different characteristics. The most obvious and the most important is how it takes a soft dark pencil. Try to find a paper that easily displays a nice black for (say) a 6B pencil lead, and does so without excessive shine. That's not the only important criteria. Some surfaces allow you to also erase cleanly. This is an important advantage so try to find a paper that allows you to erase several times without getting damaged.

Note that all paper is permanently changed by the application and removal of graphite. Usually, this is bad, but we can exploit the change in surface and resulting display of graphite to create texture and other artistic effects. Actually, any process that alters the original tooth of the paper will alter subsequent application of graphite. A good example of this is embossing or burnishing.

Shine

Since the graphite flakes are flat and shiny, rubbing a pencil hard on the paper will flatten the tooth and lay all the flakes flat on top of each other. Light will reflect off this smooth surface and cause shine. This is undesirable because a shiny surface will not properly depict a shadow. It is wise to lay down the graphite and preserve the tooth so each individual flake of graphite reflects light in a different direction. Carbon and charcoal pencils are made of rough bits of black carbon grains, and do not reflect much light even if you crush the tooth.

Some types of paper cause shine more than others. You will need to experiment to find out what suits your style. Using a fixative, and placing artwork behind glass tends to reduce but not eliminate shine. It's difficult to imagine how the property of shine could be desirable, but perhaps as features in an abstract work it might work. Normally, try to avoid the problem.

Pencil Grade

Pencils are marked with a grading system. There are two measures: B and H. Each letter could be preceded by a number which indicates a weighting for the letter. Read B as "graphite" and H as "clay". Graphite is soft and shiny, while the clay is hard and matte. On a ten-value scale from soft to hard, we get:

1. 8B
2. 6B
3. 4B
4. 2B
5. B
6. HB
6.5. F
7. H
8. 2H
9. 4H
10. 6H

On any given paper, each of these will give a very dark (8B) to very light (6H) value. For any given pencil grade, it will give a different value depending on the paper used. Some papers take darks better than others. HB is in the middle for a general-purpose pencil that we use in schools. Softer pencil marks, when used lightly are easy to erase while harder pencil marks can damage the tooth of the paper and leave an impression. Therefore, light pressure in many layers will often produce superior results when compared with heavy-handed marks. You can apply soft over hard or hard over soft layers. The two results differ, and I find that a combination of hard and soft pencils often work well for hair.

Below is the complete value scale for the following pencils in order: 6H 5H 4H 3H 2H H F HB.

Next is the complete value scale for the softer pencils:
B, 2B, 3B, 4B, 5B, 6B, 7B, 8B.

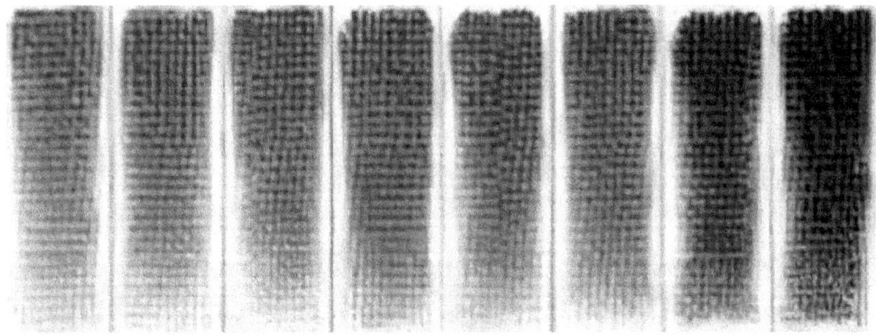

In practice, you don't need many pencils. 4H is hard enough for most tasks. Whether you need something as soft as 8B depends on the structure of the paper and tooth size, but I find even an HB can do well on the right paper. Especially considering that we have the option to use carbon and charcoal for deep darks, the softer pencils are less useful.

At least for a start, you can get by nicely with the following: 4H, H, HB, 4B.

In the USA and some other parts of the world, a different scale is in use. Here are some rough equivalents:

#1 = B

#2 = HB

#2½ = F

#3 = H

#4 = 2H

Feeling

Drawing is a visual art and it might seem strange to talk about feeling, but one of the goals of art is to induce emotion in the viewer. You can use the expression on a person's face to convey a feeling. This might be sadness, shock, tiredness and so on. Also, the background, texture, composition and the way that objects are presented will have an influence on the feeling of a picture. Colour invokes emotion but in our graphite portraits, we have only shades of grey. Although this might seem a disadvantage, it can be dramatic and deep. It is interesting that black-and-white photography was once a cheap and easy method, while colour photography was considered expensive and elite. But today, we find processes for colour photography have become mass-produced, cheap and common. Black-and-white photography is now considered dramatic, arty and elite. At the time of writing (2008–2012), graphite art is slowly making progress in the art world. Hopefully, this is because great graphite works are so capable of showing feeling. The absence of colour should be treated as an advantage to bring out the drama of a subject.

Angle

Lines which are drawn or implied and are not either horizontal or vertical create a dramatic effect. Diagonal and angled lines help to accentuate a subject or lead the eye to a specific place in the drawing. Sometimes, the diagonal lines are made from parts of the subject. Sometimes the lines will be part of the background. Use these ideas carefully—as anything that is overused becomes boring.

It's important to locate where the angles fit in your composition. For example, the jaw-line, tilt of head, and slant of mouth. These angles work together to make the picture homogeneous and each is related to the other.

Another major point to note about angles is related to curves in the following way: If you simply observe and try to copy the curve from an ear to chin, your brain will overemphasise the extent of the curve. To reproduce a curve like this, draw or imagine an angled line running along the curve. You will find the curved part is only a slight deviation from the angled line. The outline of a face is troublesome for a novice. Beginners sometimes draw cheeks that bulge too far.

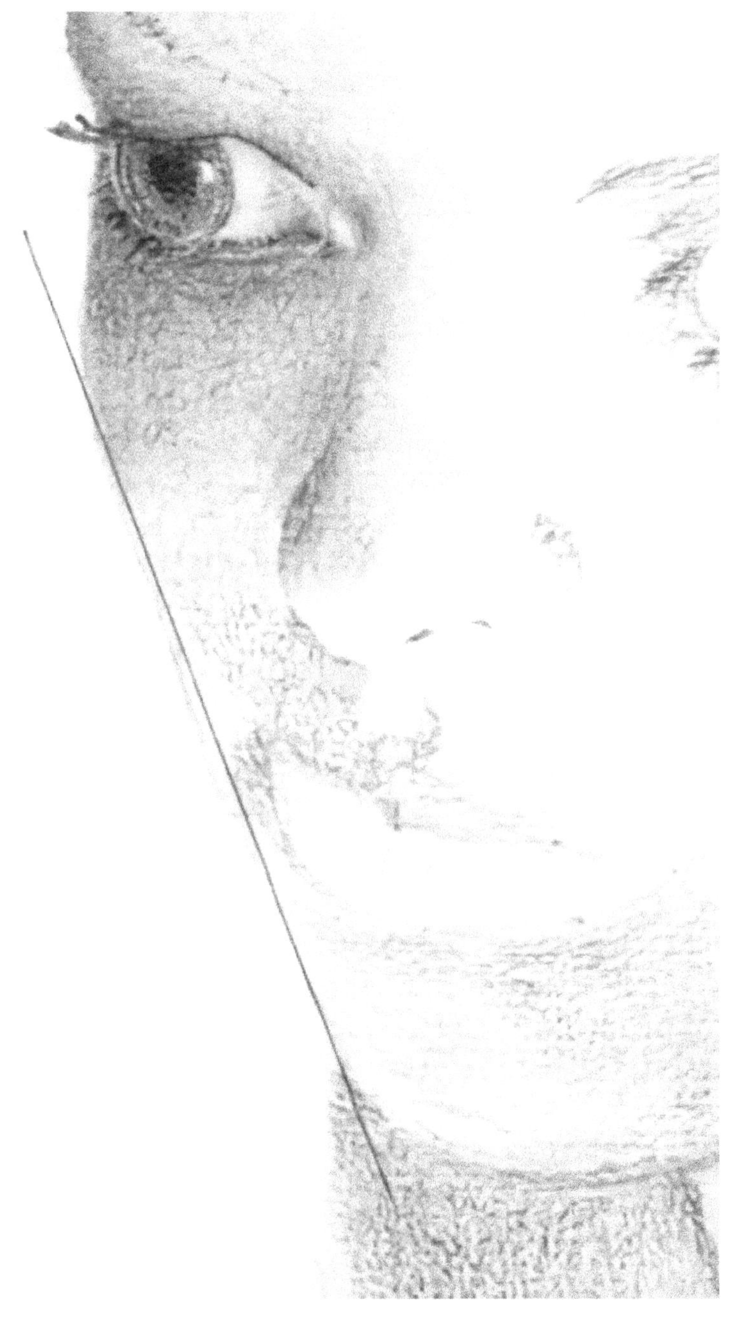

In the example sketch above, notice how slight the curve of the woman's cheek deviates from a perfect straight line. Look for these strategic lines in your portraiture references and study not so much the curve, but how little it deviates from a straight line. You can sometimes create a contour drawing of curved objects using only straight lines.

Composition

You will be able to get several books dedicated to the topic of composition, so I'll mention that it is important, and advise to find some extra literature on the subject. The purpose now is to define the term. Composition obviously comes from the verb to compose which means to put parts together into a new whole. In a picture, the parts that are available include at least the following:

Value, Colour, Shape, Angle, Focus, Blur, Detail, Texture, Emotion, Negative space, Balance...

A good composition will hold the viewer's attention, and let the eye explore the drawing and rest on the desired subject matter. All the elements should complement and enhance the subject, and there should not be two or more equally competing objects in the drawing... unless of course you want and can control this effect. It is also a good idea to arrange the objects so the viewer's eye is held within the frame. A drawing which contains an arrangement that causes the eye to leave the frame is unlikely to hold interest. Some or perhaps most people can feel a good composition when they see it even without being able to explain the theory behind it. If you can do this, take advantage of it by playing with the elements until they feel right. This is a good reason to draw several sketches before committing to a fully rendered drawing. It helps to have a point of focus in a composition and there are several ways to guide the viewer's attention to the focal point. You could use colour, focus and guides from other elements in the picture, objects that frame it, opacity and many other tools. It seems a little nebulous to say this, but it's true that a good composition is something you feel more than observe. In a good composition, there is often a primary focus while the rest of the work enhances and supports this focus in some way.

Depth

This is a term which can be used to describe several things about a drawing. Good contrast might give depth, but so might the subject matter in an emotional sense. Control of focus and all the other elements might contribute to depth. It might be easier to describe this by imagining a person who is shallow, and then one who has great depth. It's hard to put these concepts into words, but if you can imagine the person who has depth, and apply the feeling to a drawing, then this is what we are trying to understand. Depth can also be part of the history of the drawing, and of the conditions and life of the artist. Therefore some ordinary works get sold for a lot of money: the artwork is inextricably linked to a time, place, world view, political environment and the trials and tribulations of the artist. Do not overlook this important and intangible concept.

Pop

When you draw something that should be sticking out of the page, like a nose, if it looks like the feature is no longer flat, it has pop. This is achieved by careful rendering of light and shadow. Pop is a major goal for realistic portrait work. Of course, it means to create a 3D effect, but is also something more than this. Pop comes with a pleasing element of surprise or impact for the viewer.

3D

A piece of paper only has horizontal and vertical coordinates. It therefore only has two dimensions, but we can use shading, highlights, focus and blur to create the illusion of a third dimension perpendicular to the page. This really is an illusion. The paper is flat, but the mind is accustomed to seeing certain shadows and highlights in certain arrangements on a real three-dimensional surface. When we successfully emulate this in a drawing, the effect is to trick the mind into appreciating this third dimension. Part of this is simply because the sun is above, and shadows are underneath objects. A trick I like to use with portraits is to cast the shadow on the face of a lock of hair which is hovering above the surface. It is the shadow that creates an illusion of the third dimension.

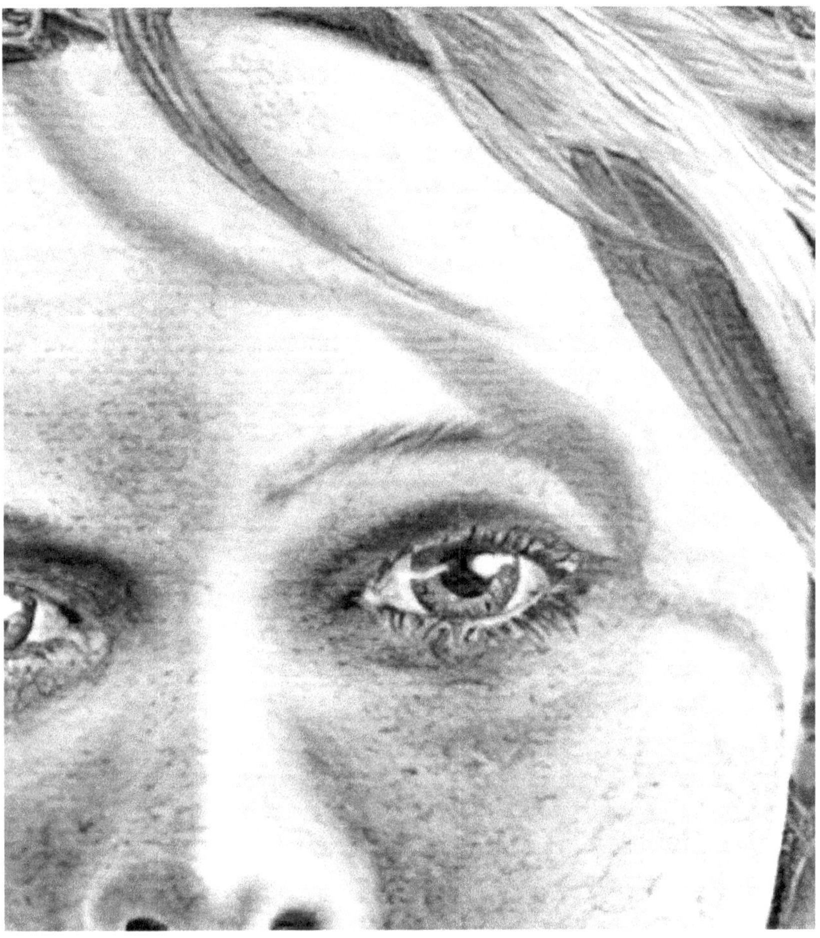

In this detail, we can see the effect of the shadow from the hair as it falls over the curves on the face, and the bright highlight on the tip of the nose. These help to give a 3D effect. Note how the eye looks spherical due to the slight curve in the highlight and mostly because of the shading in the corners.

Punching up

When you complete a drawing, all the general values have been established. The midtones should be right and all the shadows in the right place. But sometimes you need more impact. A process called punching up can improve the drawing. This is where you look for the deep shadows and try to make them blacker without losing texture and detail in the shadows. It increases drama and contrast.

Blending

When you put graphite onto the paper, you often want a smooth transition from dark to light. In one technique, (circularism), this is achieved without blending. The results are nice, but the process is slow. Many people like to use a tool like a rag or tissue to move the graphite around on the paper to achieve a smooth result. Blending is to take a non-drawing instrument and use it to smudge the graphite. Depending on the paper, the grade of pencil, and the blending tool, you get different results. Here are some commonly used tools:

- Tissue.
- Stump.
- Paper.
- Rag.
- Fur
- Paintbrush.
- Tortillon.
- Chamois.

Blending is a compromise in some ways. Particularly in the midvalues, when you blend your marks some liveliness is lost. However, it works well for smooth skin, like that of a small child. It is also useful for hair, and as a layered application to achieve deep darks without breaking the paper's tooth. You need to experiment with blending. Sometimes it works, sometimes not, and you can also use it as one technique in a multilayered approach. For example, make some marks, blend them, use an eraser, or other pencil grades to make texture, then either blend again or glaze with a hard pencil and so on. Try blending over highlights and use an eraser to pull the highlights back selectively.

Lifting

Once you lay graphite on paper, you often want to remove completely some of it. If so, an eraser used in the conventional way will work fine. However, lifting graphite rather than rubbing it away will take off the top layer or so leaving a more even and subdued result. You might add another layer or continue to lift graphite until it looks right. You can also lift parts of a shape to mimic how values reduce as the lighting reflects across the surface. Use a kneadable eraser to do this.

Layers

In the same way that you use multiple layers of paint to protect a door or produce an oil painting, multiple layers of graphite will improve your drawing. You might put one layer down as dots or circles in HB, followed by a glaze of 6H, then some dots or strokes with B, then strokes with H followed by some lifting and more layers. The result will be much more interesting than a single layer of graphite. Layering is a good way to build realistic texture. Use different pencil grades or different marks in each layer for best effect.

Fringing and shadows

If you hold an object against a light source, you will find that its perimeter does not look like a solid and abrupt transition from light to shadow. Light leaks around the edge because the edge is not perfect. I call this fringing. Consequently, the shadow that is cast by the object does not have a hard edge.

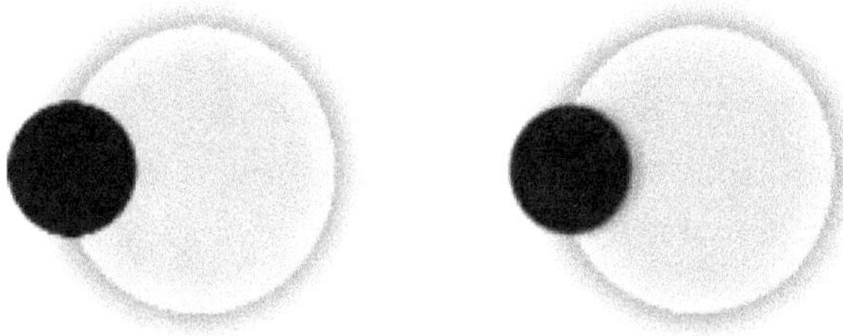

Therefore, you should not draw hard edges in shadows—partly for this reason, and mainly because of reflected incident light. In the exaggerated example above the larger object is a source of light. The illustration on the left is drawn naively, while the one on the right supports the observation that the edge is somewhat 'lost' due to the back-lighting.

Halo effect

Fringing causes something like a halo effect, but there are two more interesting cases. One is caused by simultaneous contrast. When two strong contrasting colours are juxtaposed, they almost fight for dominance at the boundary. Scientists noted this, and so did artists, leading to the definition, "The spontaneous spreading of colour beyond its actual realm." In practice, this means you can join two highly contrasting colours at a sharp boundary, and yet perceive a smeared transition.

Another source of halation comes from flaws in early photographic chemistry. Early film would bleed light beyond its proper boundaries when it was developed. Sometimes this is used for artistic effect in a beauty-shot or other moody picture. The effect is particularly noticeable with back-lit scenes.

To anchor this development in history, let's note by 1430, images could be projected using concave mirrors. By 1600 lenses gave better images. By 1650 we have the camera obscura.

A Dutch realist artist, Jan Vermeer lived from 1632–1675. In Vermeer's work, and in particular "Girl with a red hat", art historians note a possible—but disputed—link between film-halation and his technique with painting light. Although Vermeer did not appear to own a camera obscura, some of his paintings suggest he deliberately used a halo-effect.

In most cases halation in film is annoying and it's certain by 1904 chemists created an antihalation layer for film. Today, you will buy a film with antihalation by default but can also ask for one without.

Reflected light sources

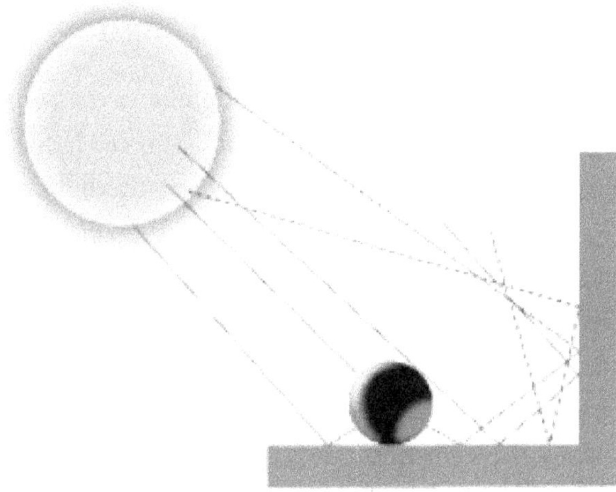

Assume the big ball in the top left in the above illustration is a light source. Rays of light are emitted from this in all directions. I've shown a few of these, and done some manual imaginary 'ray-tracing' to try to work out what happens to them. Some hit the ball perpendicular to it. This is where you will find the highest highlight. Some hit the floor in front of the ball and bounce up and illuminate it underneath. Many beginners incorrectly draw the ball as if the unlit side is in shadow. However, depending on the reflective quality of the floor, some light will bounce back onto the object. This creates a second highlight. This highlight cannot be as bright at the major one unless the floor is a perfect mirror. Rays of light bounce off the wall at the right, then to the floor at the rear, and to the object from behind. This creates a third highlight but it is much less intense than the other two because a) the wall absorbed some energy and b) the floor absorbed further energy.

Additionally, light sources are not infinitely tiny. They have significant dimension which means that a light source sends rays of light past the object from many angles. This means the intensity of a shadow is greatest where most light-rays are blocked, and becomes weaker as you move away from that spot.

The components of a shadow

A typical light source—like that from a globe or passing through a window—cannot be thought of as a point-source. It has significant dimension. This means that different parts of the light source cause significantly different angles of light-rays to fall on the object. The only way to avoid this is to either have a light source infinitely tiny, or infinitely far away. Both are unattainable—even ignoring that light falls off with the square of the distance. (I will explain this next).

However, outside in the sunlight, with no other objects around to make reflections, the light-rays arrive *almost* parallel. This is because the sun is far away and approximates a point-source. The same is true for light reflected off the moon. This surprising fact is seen in a landscape of moonlight over the water.

Naive drawings of the moonlight over water often depict the reflections with perspective that you might find looking down railway lines. But as you can see from this example, ignoring distortion from the moving water, the overall profile of the moon's reflection is parallel.

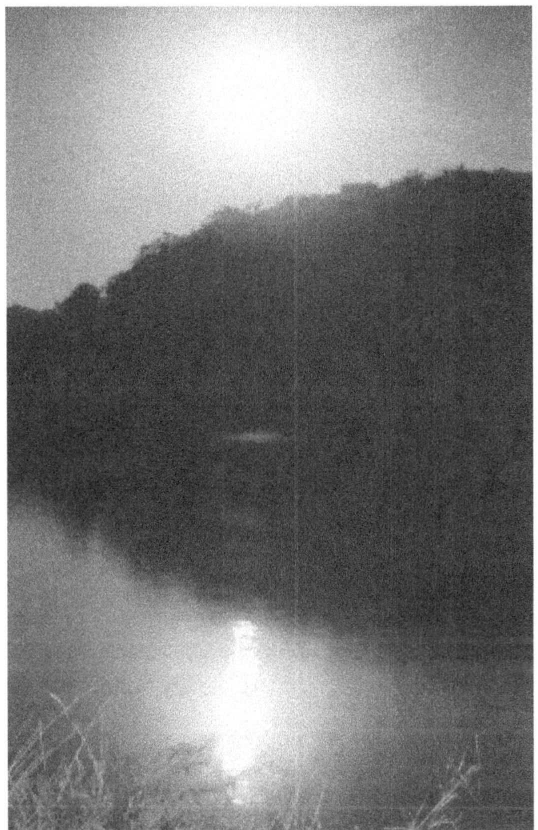

This is in contrast to nearby non-point-sources of light. If the light is like a nearby light bulb, the rays of light from different parts of the bulb are not parallel. In this case, a shadow has several identifiable components.

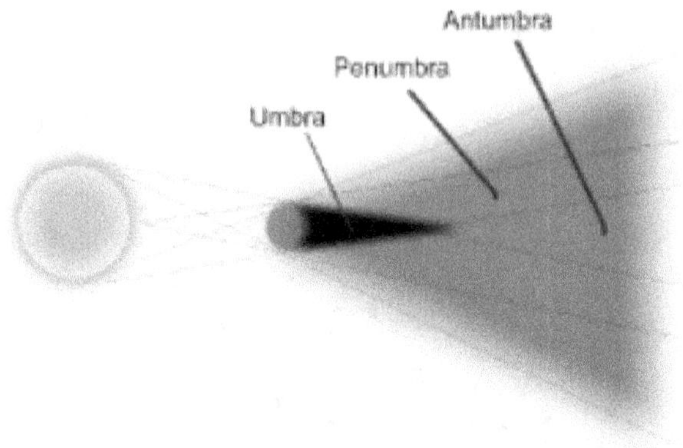

Shadows from a non-point-like source have three main components: The umbra (darkest) which receives no rays of light but tails off to a point, those same rays are mixed with rays from ambient light to create the antumbra, and finally, the penumbra where partial light is received. Don't worry too much about this technical description; just be aware that most shadows have a structure. Train yourself to look for this kind of thing when observing your reference, especially when your subject is wholly or partially backlit.

Shadow dilution

When there is only a single light source, shadows do not get darker where they overlap. But when you have multiple light sources as in the example below, an object will cast multiple shadows. Some shadows get diluted. In other words, they get lighter. This is nicely illustrated in the picture below of a cup on a white table where the windows acted like multiple light sources. Note the position of the darkest shadow.

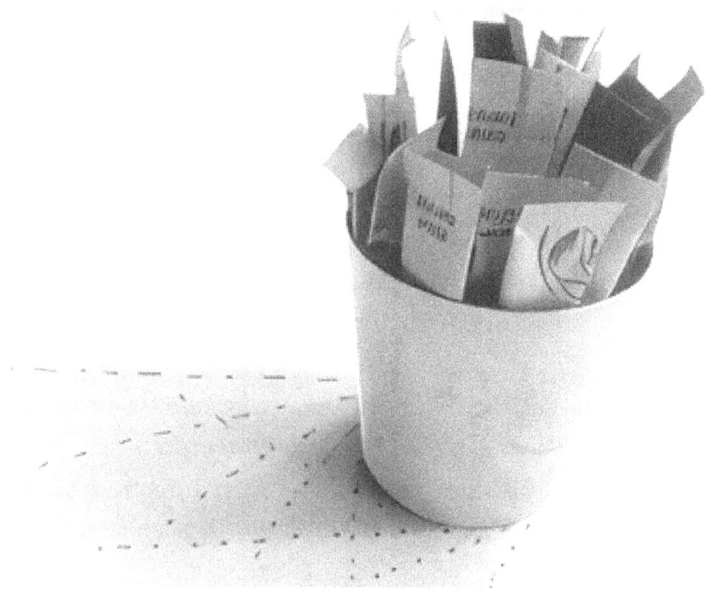

When you begin to draw portraits with multiple light sources, or near strong reflective surfaces, you will need to take special note of the complexity of shadows in the face. If done correctly, the result is engaging.

With distance, light becomes weak quickly

In physics, it is common to hear the statement, "Light falls off with the square of the distance." While that is usually easy to understand for a physics student, it might be a little obscure to many. Imagine a ball, into which you place skewers until there is no more surface area left. You could count the skewers inserted into one square centimetre of the ball—let's assume you counted twenty. Now count the number of skewers passing through a 1cm square area one centimetre distance away from the ball's surface. You expect intuitively to count fewer because they radiate outwards. Each time you move a centimetre away, the number of skewers counted for a square-centimetre is dramatically fewer. This is what happens with light-rays. If a source of light is of brightness 256 (The units do not matter), then at some distance further you will measure only 16, and the same distance away again, you will measure 4, then 2, then 1.4 then only 1.1 and so on. This is why your small built-in camera flash is ineffective for large groups of people.

Now that you understand how light spreads out, try to use this idea in your drawings. If you have a single light-source that illuminates an object that is supposed to have depth into the page, take account of how quickly the object becomes dark further from the source of light.

Sfumato—or transition

In oil painting, sfumato is achieved using a dry brush. In pencil drawing, we try to emulate the effect.

In the quest for realism, sfumato is a powerful tool. Its roots are in classical painting. Leonardo da Vinci invented the technique; art historian Ernst Gombrich reveals the famous enigmatic smile of the Mona Lisa is due to sfumato at the corner of her mouth. The viewer is tantalizingly held on a precipice between raising one of two questions. "Is it a smile?" or "Is it a shadow?"

See also the description for scumbling as this is closely related.

The corner of a person's mouth is an interesting area for a portrait artist. The slightest variation is detected by the viewer, and can have a profound effect on the person's expression. Additionally, the corner of the mouth is not so much where the lips end, but where they fade into cheek. This fade is complicated by the flexibility of tiny muscles in that area. Depending on how these muscles pull, the transition from dark to light in this area will vary. If you draw an outline for the lips, it might work for the upper and lower edge but joining those two edges at the corner of the mouth looks awful. This is where sfumato comes in. You need to suggest the edge but not draw it. You need to move gradually but convincingly from a dark tone to a lighter tone, and make due consideration for a dimple or slight asymmetry from one side of the mouth to the other. These tiny variations are extremely important to properly render a convincing realistic portrait. Above, I mentioned that an outline for the upper and lower lips "sort of works". You can get away with a drawn-edge for the lips, but will get better realism using sfumato. Lipstick will complicate the use of sfumato, because it may create a false edge and possibly also allow the real edge to be still mildly visible. Lipstick needs a quicker transition while natural lips have a more subtle and wider transition. This is especially true for wrinkles and the boundary between the face and the background. Even if something is drawn onto the face—like a clown's makeup, the natural texture of the skin will smear the edge.

Sfumato is useful for creases in clothes, and on the neck. Ignoring this can lead to an unconvincing portrait.

Glaze

A rounded and smooth point on a hard-grade pencil produces a light but consistent mark on the paper. If you use this over the top of other layers of graphite, and make it cover the whole area consistently, we call it a glaze. It fills in little gaps and inconsistencies. It tends to unify the rendering. This transforms a drawing because it no longer looks like raw pencil marks. It fills the entire tooth on the paper, leaving no stark white dots and often this step makes a good pencil portrait look to some people like a photograph.

Oils (In skin)

Try to avoid touching the paper. Some techniques will cause fingerprints and oily smudges to give an inconsistent finish. Some areas of your drawing will suffer if you don't have perfect control over the values. For example, a smooth cheek won't look good if an oily fingerprint causes the graphite to be darker in one area. Other areas are not so sensitive, like the foliage of a tree, or an area in the hair.

Graphite dust acts like a fingerprint-detector as fine particles stick to the oils in our skin. Over a long time, previously invisible oil can discolour the paper.

Embossing

Embossing is an interesting and sometimes extremely useful technique for preserving fine highlights. A good example is dark hair where there are numerous small hairs which reflect light. An embossing tool could be a knitting-needle type metal point. You need it fine but smooth. The idea is to compress the tooth of the paper and subsequent layers won't fill the compressed area.

Burnishing

Burnishing is to rub a surface with a hard smooth object like the back of a spoon. It will alter, but not scratch the surface. To experiment with burnishing, take a sample of paper, and a teaspoon. Burnish an area, and apply different strokes and grades of pencil to the burnished and non-burnished areas. Try to get a feel for how this affects the paper.

Recall this in future in case it produces an effect or texture that you find difficult to obtain otherwise. It could work well with techniques involving graphite dust. A word of caution: burnishing cannot be undone.

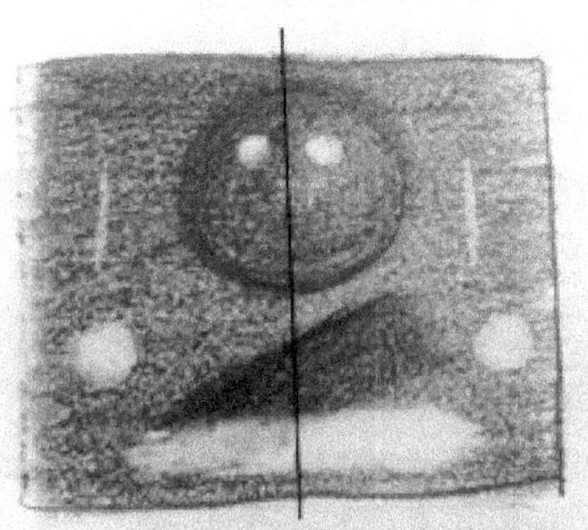

In the picture here, the rectangle on the right was lightly burnished by using the back of a stainless-steel spoon. This flattened the tooth. The same stroke and techniques were applied to both left and right rectangles. The major differences are: Grain is more apparent on the left. The marks are darker on the left. Surprisingly, erasing the burnished area is easier.

If you burnish paper, it will take the pencil marks differently to untouched paper. However, you should be in the position to choose when to do this. Don't do it accidentally, and avoid poor quality paper which might have burnished spots.

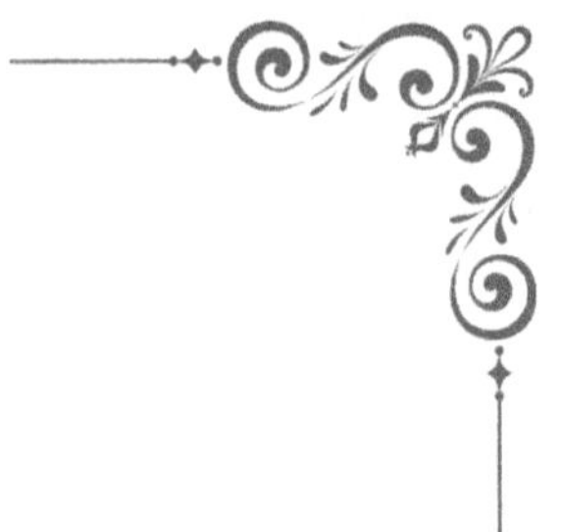

Tools

Smudge mask

On a large work, you might need to rest your hand on the paper while drawing. A smudge mask helps to reduce or prevent smudging from your arm. A normal piece of paper works well, but greaseproof paper or baking paper as used in cooking works better because it is slightly slippery and less likely to raise graphite from your drawing. It's easy to rip, so you can tape some baking paper over your work, cut a hole in the middle, and progressively rip it away as you need to expose more of your drawing. It's also slightly transparent which is useful because you can see some preparatory marks beneath.

Paper

Paper comes in a bewildering range. Quality and characteristics vary with price. You must purchase acid-free paper. This is because normal paper as you might use in a printer reacts with light. The manufacturing process is tuned for profit and to produce a product fit for the purpose. Ordinary copy-paper does not need to have archival properties.

Acid neutralisation is an added manufacturing expense. Therefore, normal paper typically has a small amount of acid in it which reacts over time with the environment and turns yellow. Artists' paper is nearly acid-free and this is a big advantage for long-term exhibition. Not only must your paper be acid-free, but so too the mat board used to frame your work.

Most white papers are only white to your eye when there is nothing whiter to compare. You will find there are many shades, some "whiter" than others. Some are beige, some slightly yellow and so on.

Paper also comes in different texture grades. Very smooth paper is good for high detail but it can be difficult to make a black mark, while you may prefer a rougher tooth for a different look.

You can burnish parts of the paper to simulate a smooth paper but doing so limits its ability to take dark marks.

Especially if you are doing a series, or a triptych, it's important to be consistent. Sometimes the paper is smooth on one side, and rough on the other. In that case, it's best to mark the paper with a small cross in the top right corner on the side that you choose to use.

Paper comes in different thicknesses (also called weight). Obviously, the higher the weight, the thicker, and more robust is the paper. Thin paper might be smooth, but easily creased. Another overlooked characteristic of paper is how easily it allows an eraser to work.

Different paper reacts differently to moisture. Some will crinkle and stain, while specialist watercolour papers are more stable.

Finally, various surfaces take pencil differently so the blackest black you can get on one paper might be considerably darker on another.

For these reasons, you should experiment. Only your own preference and experience can help you choose the right paper for a given style and subject.

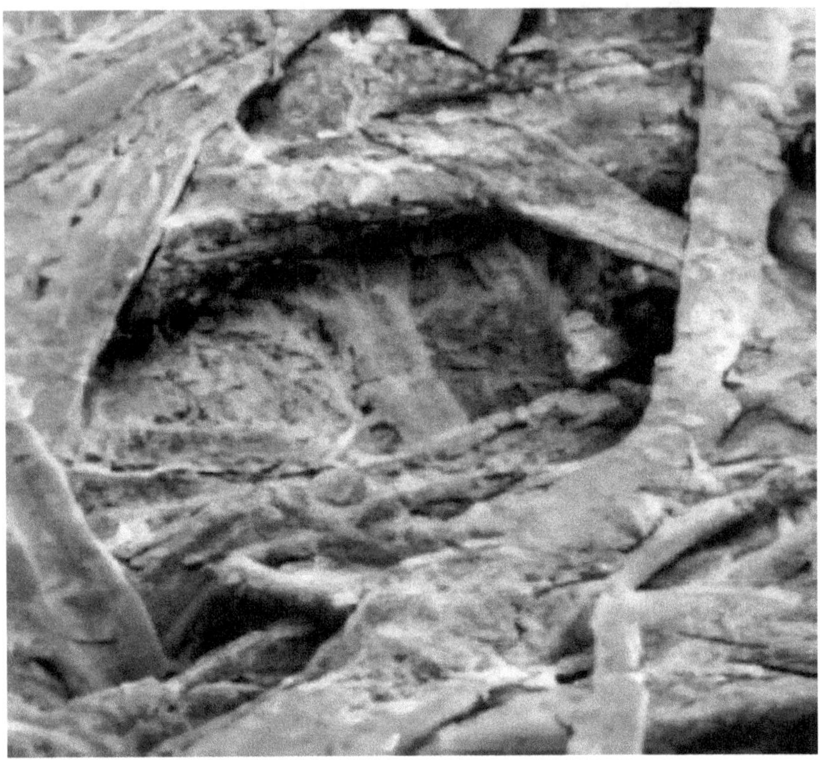

One micrometre is one millionth of a metre. The picture above is blown up from a square of paper about 100 micrometres across. You can clearly see what we call tooth, peaks and valleys. The tooth refers to the roughness. A valley is like a crater in the surface and the peaks are the tops of the fibres. It's important to appreciate that different paper has different physical characteristics. Large particles will not fit into the valleys. Blunt pencils will deposit graphite only on the tops, while a sharp hard pencil is likely to break up these grains and force them into the valleys.

For a given set of pencils, a specific technique will have a different effect on different paper. Each paper has a tooth-size, and there will be a particular grade of pencil that nicely fills the valleys of the tooth. It's useful for any given type of paper to find out what grade of pencil does this because a flake-size which just fills the tooth is like a benchmark for that paper. It will give you an easy convincing dark without too much shine, and if used lightly, is less likely to give a grainy effect. Use a soft pencil for a deliberate grainy effect, and a hard one to prepare the paper for a controlled layering of softer pencil on top.

Pressing a tool hard damages the tooth. The effects you get depend not only on the particular paper, but also the pencil grade and its shape, and how hard you press.

An appreciation of the structure of paper also gives you some insight into how various blending techniques work. Some paper is made from tough fibres while others are weak. Weak fibres are likely to break which will affect your work method and results—especially when using an eraser.

If paper were perfectly smooth, you would not be able to make a mark on it with graphite because it would not be abrasive enough to tear away graphite from the pencil.

Since the size of graphite flakes varies with different grades of pencil, the combination of pencil-choice and tooth is significant. Soft graphite has comparatively big flakes, and—as noted—sits on top of the paper's tooth, not in the valleys. A hard pencil will be able to fill the valleys, but will not be dark.

You can get different effects by choosing the order or layering. Here is the reason: Soft big graphite flakes are slippery (and shiny), so a hard pencil used over a soft layer will break up the flakes, force them into the valleys, and the peaks will shave off the harder graphite. Hard pencils over soft layers work well. For the opposite, if you first lay down a hard layer, then because it fills the valleys and covers the peaks, and is slippery, a soft grade is less likely to go on top. Contrary to some of my research, where it is said that you should only apply hard over soft, I think each is a legitimate technique. If you lay down a soft layer lightly first, some paper will still show through, leaving a grainy appearance. The harder pencil on top will therefore enhance this because it will adhere less to the flakes of graphite that are already there, and stick well to the exposed parts of the tooth. You should try this and note the result. Compare this with putting down a gentle layer of hard pencil, and applying soft over the top. In this case, you don't get the grainy appearance, and instead get a nice smooth result. This technique will not get it as dark.

When you make a transition from dark to light, and would like a smooth result, the dark areas need to be done with soft: layer-blend-layer-blend-layer. For the lighter areas use hard then soft pencils. Blending is optional depending on the look that you want. In the transition area where it is not the darkest, and not into the "hard then soft" area, you need to mix the technique.

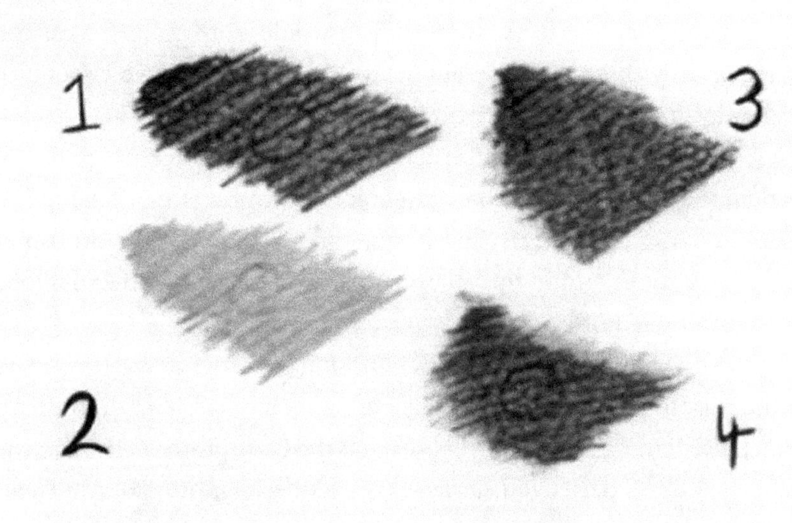

In the experiment:

#1: I used a soft pencil for the base then drew a circle on top using the same pencil.

#2: I used a hard pencil for the base then drew a circle on top using the same pencil.

#3: I used a hard layer over a soft layer and then a hard pencil to try to make a circle but it would not make a mark.

#4: I used a soft layer over a hard layer then a soft pencil to make the circle.

Consistency

Like many other products, paper is mass-produced. It is made from wood pulp, and other additives. The quality of the pulp, the quality of the tools and processes, and cleanliness of the environment are important. Cheap paper will be made in an inferior way, often with hard bits, contaminants, and sometimes holes. These inconsistencies might not show until you try to put a layer of graphite on it. More expensive paper is worth the price because the chance of getting a poor spot is reduced. It is still possible to get bad paper that is sold as good quality, but the event is rare. I've read anecdotal reports which claim that paper sold in a block-pad is more consistent than loose sheets. Why this should be so is a mystery to me, but worth mentioning as the information has come from several sources.

Hot press paper

Hot press paper is formed by squeezing the paper through hot rollers. This makes a smooth surface. Since it has little tooth, this means it is less abrasive which often means more difficulty to get dark non-shiny shadows. Its smooth surface is good for fine detail. When you need to create a texture-effect, then you need to build the texture with layers using differing techniques and pencil grades. Hot press paper can often be more expensive than cold press paper for a given weight and size. The smooth surface is good for making copies and preserving fine detail.

Hot press board often comes in bright-white or with a coated surface. The advantage of bright-white paper is potentially greater dynamic range. However, on a smooth or coated surface, it might be difficult to create dark areas. As usual, once you find a supplier, it is a good idea to test the paper with a quick sketch. If you like the bright white and the coated surface but have difficulty getting a deep dark, consider using a carbon pencil.

A bright white paper might be difficult to reproduce onto normal paper, so the original is likely to look much better than copies. The bright white paper can also cause significant problems to get even illumination for photographic reproduction and display. If you have made some fine art that you would like to reproduce well, consider the giclée process. Giclée prints were originally created on a specific printer called an IRIS printer, which is a high-resolution, high-format industrial prepress proofing inkjet machine. Today, the word implies fade-resistant, archival inks on archival-quality substrates and used in any of several brands of inkjet printer.

Cold press paper

Cold press paper may also be called "Not Hot" or simply, "Not". It has more tooth than hot press paper which makes fine detail more difficult, but is a better surface for deep darks with less shine. When you need to create a texture-effect, the tooth of the paper can be exploited by choosing various pencil grades and pressure.

Mat board

Mat board is readily available because it is used for mounts around a picture in a frame. It is acid-free. Mat board usually has significant texture. It's difficult to work on for beginners and it might be a little delicate compared with high quality paper. This means that it will not "take the layers" as well. However, some artists like mat board for graphite. If you use it, be very gentle with the pencils. Use only the weight of the pencil to make a mark, and be patient.

Illustration board

Illustration board is finished only on one side. The good side is often watermarked in one corner and can serve as an indicator if you are in doubt. If you cut down a full sheet, place a small identifier on the good side to make it easy to identify later.

The surface of an illustration board is good for digital scanning and as a master for print making. If you intend to reproduce your original art and sell copies, consider illustration board—if it suits your style.

Bristol board

Bristol board has two working surfaces. It is often lighter than illustration board. It is good for long-term use and preserves well. You can also find archival Bristol board.

Plate Bristol board

Plate Bristol board is somewhat like hot press.

Vellum

Vellum Bristol board is somewhat like cold press.

Drafting paper

Drafting paper is an interesting support. It is smooth, yet rough which is an odd thing to state, but I mean by this that it seems smooth to touch, but when you draw on it, it grabs the graphite and wears the pencil quickly. It's almost like extremely fine sandpaper. Because of this, it produces a good black. Another interesting property is that it is translucent. For beginners, this is an advantage if you care to copy a picture on a scale of 1:1. Simply overlay the drawing, and trace a contour. Then you can place the drafting paper on a clear white background and progress to do rendering. When you use an eraser, it will smudge. It will also smudge when touching it, however these smudges will vanish with a clean eraser, and the surface is tough. It's an unusual but interesting option for graphite artists.

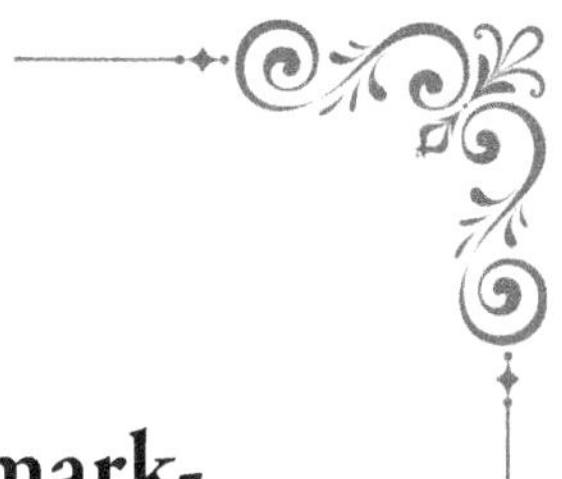

Pencils and other mark-making tools

Wooden pencils

There is definitely a wide quality-range for wooden pencils. The main difference is consistency. You need the graphite core to be devoid of hard scratchy bits, and places where it breaks easily. Obviously hard pencils don't break easily, but they may contain scratchy bits. These scratchy bits can damage the paper. Soft pencils can be easily broken, so as well as careful sharpening, you need good quality construction because if the lead is fragile, it becomes difficult to sharpen. The wooden casing also needs to be soft yet consistent. It should be easy to remove with a knife without putting undue strain on the core. You will need to purchase various brands to find out their characteristics, or get some recommendations from someone who has already gained the experience.

When you sharpen a wooden pencil, it is useful to shave off a lot of wood to expose a long core. Use a knife rather than a pencil sharpener because you have a lot more control, and a sharpener is wasteful. The point that a sharpener creates wears quickly, and you need to use it often. It's useful to keep some fine sandpaper in your toolkit to hone the tip. If you do this, keep the graphite dust in a small tin because it's useful as a drawing medium. Do not inhale graphite dust.

Mechanical pencils

Mechanical pencils are the tool of choice for many graphite artists. Some prefer wooden cases because they can shape the lead and produce a wide variety of marks but a mechanical pencil uses a small cylinder of graphite which is consistent in diameter and quality. They come in various diameters: 0.5mm, 0.7mm, 0.9mm and larger. I prefer the 0.5mm size because most of my portraits are small and this allows fine detail. If you are covering large areas, larger leads will improve speed but make a wider mark. The mechanical pencils can be cheap or surprisingly expensive. The cheap ones are almost always made of light plastic, while the expensive ones are heavier in the hand. Both have advantages. The cheap ones are light which gives you a lot of control over very delicate marks. Hold the pencil right at the end between thumb and forefinger. Cheap mechanical pencils might not grip the lead well, so if you apply significant pressure, the lead can slip back inside. However, since the techniques that we use do not involve heavy pressure, this is not a particular disadvantage for us. The expensive pencils are less easy to control for light marks because of their weight, but a consistent heavier mark can be made by using the same pencil-hold as with a light cheap pencil. As with any quality tool, they are a pleasure to use. I have one expensive mechanical pencil, and several cheap ones.

Charcoal

Charcoal is burned wood, heated in a restricted oxygen environment. A common kind of tree used for charcoal is willow. These come in short, slightly twisted sticks. You will find them soft. They make a nice matte black mark which can be expressive, good for large areas and consistent blocking. Charcoal does not adhere well to the paper, and it will not draw over the top of graphite. This is both an advantage and a disadvantage. By making graphite marks first, you can make charcoal marks over the top and leave the graphite exposed. This is useful for some textures, and sometimes dark hair. Since it does not stick well to the paper, it is easily disturbed and lifted. Once you are satisfied with the position of the charcoal, it is advisable to use a spray fixative.

Charcoal's lack of adhesion can be an advantage. It's is easy to push around over the paper, and easy to lift with an eraser. You can draw over it with graphite if required. As a simple twig, this natural product is understandably inconsistent in quality. There are hard scratchy parts in it sometimes. If this is a problem, drag the charcoal across a rough surface—perhaps a stone. This will abrade away the scratchy part.

A different product is compressed charcoal. This is still a natural product but it has been manufactured using pressure. Compressed charcoal is harder, more consistent, matte, and adheres better to the paper. Whether you choose to use compressed charcoal or natural will depend on your preference, mood, and subject. As always—experiment with the medium to get a feel for its characteristics. Try this on different paper too. You will find that carbon has a warm-black tint, while graphite is a silvery grey.

Carbon pencils

Carbon is a little like charcoal because it is the result of burning something. You may also know of something called lampblack. This is the soot that accumulates on the glass of an old-style burning lamp. It is sticky, dark, and matte.

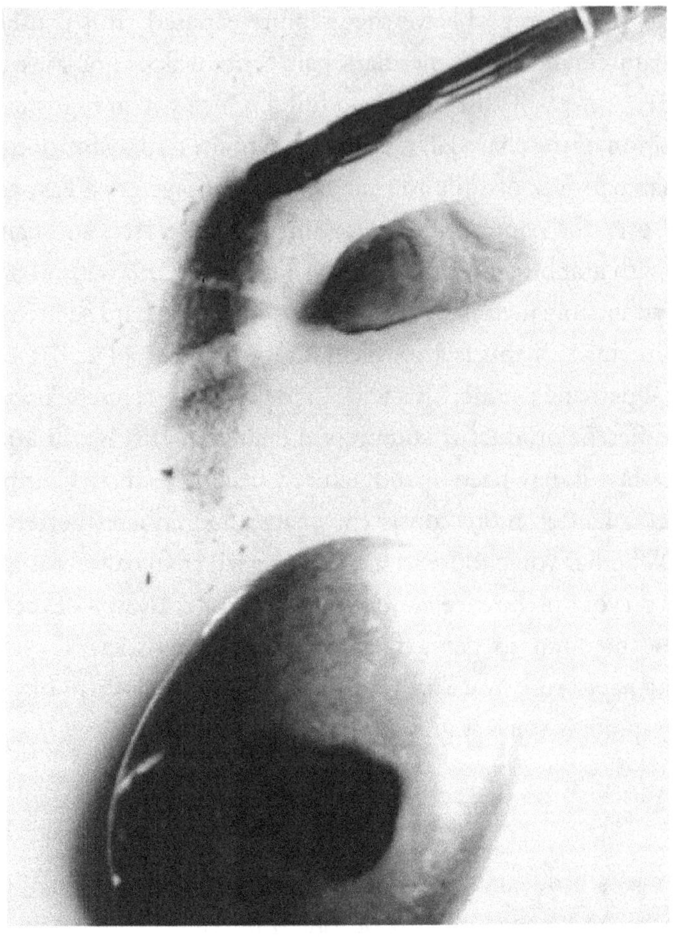

You can make your own lampblack simply by holding an old spoon over the top of a paraffin candle flame. It creates a dark sticky dust that you can paint onto your drawing surface. As you can see from the photograph below, it makes a lovely non-shiny black but it is difficult to erase. It does well for shadow areas.

I found two manufacturers that use a formula with carbon to make a wooden pencil. These two happen to have different properties even though they are both called carbon pencils. The first type I bought is scratchy sometimes, and when I put a mark on the paper it crumbled to dust. I found blowing this dust marked the paper as it skidded across.

Graphite went on top of it, but it would not mark on top of the graphite. The second type was smoother, a little less messy, and worked on top of graphite. If you choose to use carbon pencils, experiment with them and discover their characteristics. I use each one in different ways for various effects. Both of them produce a matte dark deep black that is not achievable using graphite alone. Even if you press hard and flatten the tooth, the result has no shine. Many artists find it difficult to unify the look of carbon with that of graphite but if you can manage it, the wide dynamic range is pleasingly high-impact.

Dirty eraser

As you use a kneadable eraser, it collects graphite. As it does this, it becomes less effective at lifting graphite off the paper. This can be used to your advantage. While a new piece of kneadable eraser will lift even heavy applications almost back to bare paper, a dirty one is useful for adding highlights to already-rendered areas without losing texture. To do this, roll it into a ball, flatten one side and gently dab at your drawing without rubbing the paper. You can also roll it into a tear-shape and gently dab without re-forming the tip. The tip will become saturated with graphite and gradually lose the ability to lift any more. By doing this, you can influence the gradation of a transition and add a certain amount of texture at the same time.

A hard plastic eraser gets dirty quickly—especially if you don't use much pressure because it is abrasion that "cleans" the plastic eraser by rolling off its surface. Once you have a dirty eraser, you can draw with it! For a few marks, you can use the dirty eraser to draw a blurry out-of-focus mark which could be useful in several circumstances. For example, hair that is further behind, and out of focus could be drawn with a dirty eraser. You could also use it as a first layer, or to smear existing graphite to create a feeling of motion-blur. Graphite that is laid onto the paper using this method, using gentle blending, or dust, is easy to lift. It's a good base layer where you use an eraser to create finely detailed highlights on the next layer.

Dirty tortillon

A tortillon is used for blending, but as it becomes dirty, it will draw on the paper similar to the dirty eraser as described on the previous page. The marks are soft, fuzzy, easily erased and will not crush the tooth unless you press very hard.

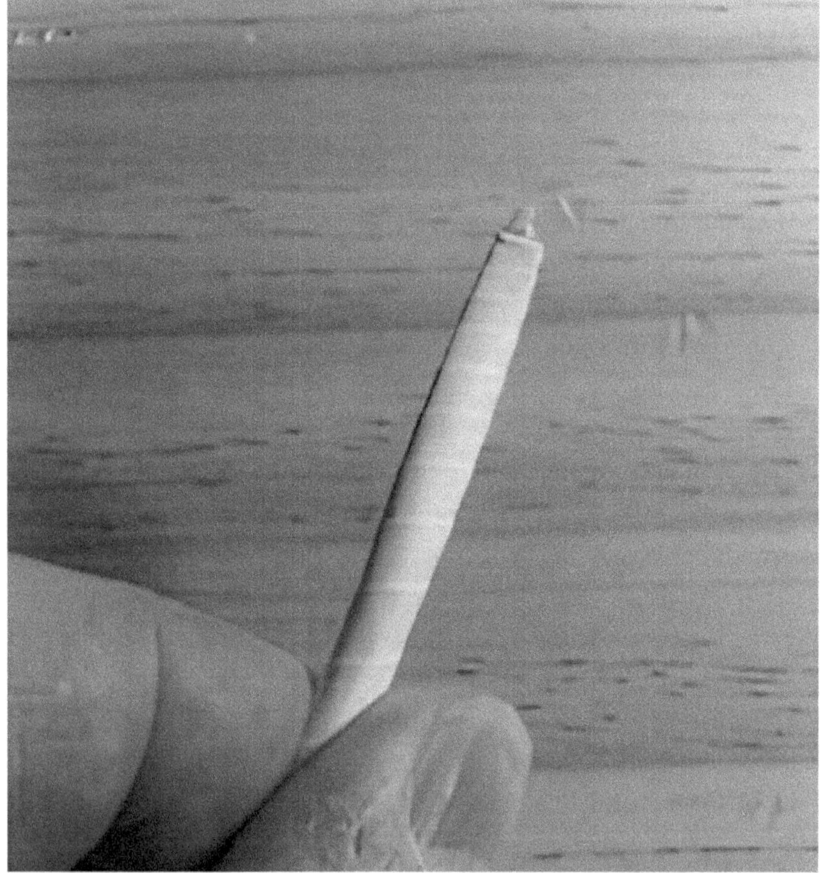

This is a homemade tortillon. It's a loosely rolled piece of paper. You can also try to roll it tight or buy one.

Paintbrush

Use a small paintbrush for blending. You get a different result with soft and hard bristles. Even a soft brush has a remarkable effect on the marks. Do not underestimate the change that you are about to make when blending with a brush. It gently spreads the graphite, and moves it deep into the tooth of the paper without crushing the tooth. It also tends to mute detail and deepen the tone more than you might expect. Use this technique in backgrounds, as first layers, and as part of the technique to get deep shadows with repeated application of graphite and blending.

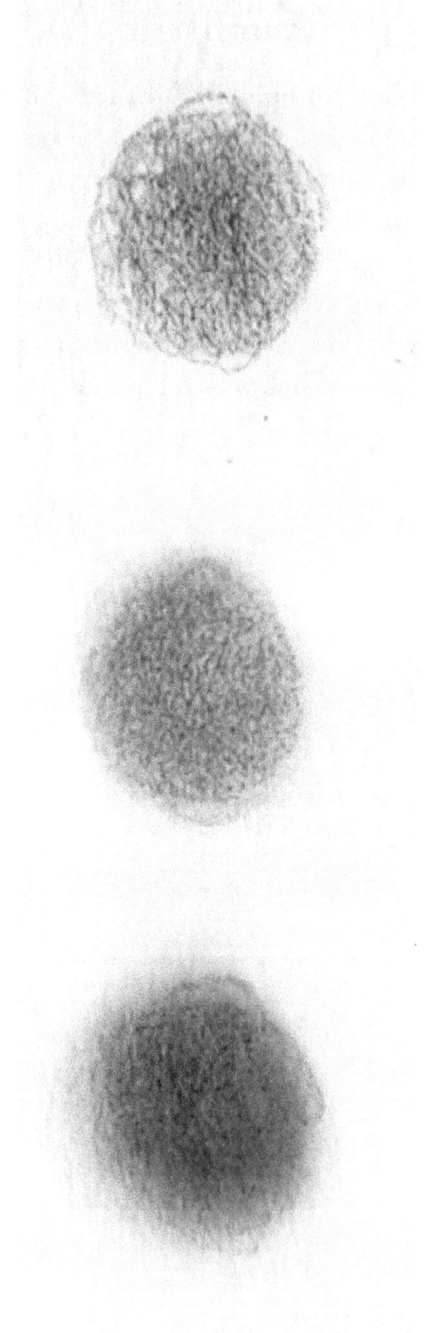

The top sample is an unblended application of a 2B pencil. The middle has been gently blended with a tortillon, and the bottom one blended with a small watercolour paintbrush. Note how the middle one leaves some of the valleys without graphite, while the paintbrush fully fills the grain of the paper. Both blending techniques obscure the original pencil marks.

Graphite dust

Graphite dust or powder may be purchased from an art supplier, or you can make your own. To make your own, obtain some glass paper (sandpaper) and grind a pencil lead into dust. Then put the dust into a small screw-top pot. Avoid breathing the dust.

The dust is applied with any of the tools used for blending or even an eraser made dirty with the dust. A paintbrush is an obvious applicator. On that note, you can also obtain liquid lead which is a commercial preparation of graphite suspended in a solvent. It seems reasonable to include this reference here, but I declare it outside the scope of this book since it is not a technique that I have tried. If you would like to experiment, you could even make your own. The solvent will need to be non-toxic and leave no stain.

Hard point for embossing

As already noted, if you make deep enough grooves, a layer of graphite or charcoal applied over the top will not fill them. It's magical to see the previously invisible marks show up. This technique has been seen in TV cop-shows where the suspect's notepad has been left at a crime scene; the detective takes a pencil and scribbles over the paper left behind to reveal what was written in the layer above.

Embossing takes planning because it is difficult to see where you have embossed before putting the graphite layer on top. It is possible to get around this by using a bright directional desk lamp held at a shallow angle. Alternatively, use tracing paper and draw heavy marks with a fine ballpoint pen, then remove the tracing paper.

Embossing on white paper will preserve white marks despite all the layers that follow. To darken an embossed mark, fill it using a very sharp pencil or perhaps work in the graphite using a soft brush.

You can apply this technique before any graphite is used, or after one or more layers. Applying the technique between layers will make half-tone highlights. With this idea, you can emboss with the full range of tones. The technique was useful for this small (15cm) drawing. The layered embossing technique was used in his beard.

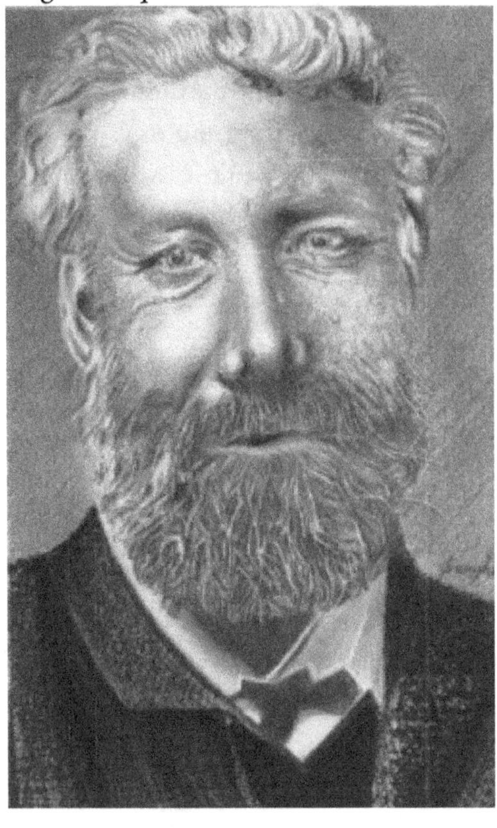

Conventional eraser

There are scores of conventional erasers available. Some are novelty types in the shape of dinosaurs and houses. Some are marketed with high claims about their efficiency. The best advice I can offer is to buy a selection ranging from cheap to more expensive, and experiment on your various papers. Even the cheap novelty type might be useful. We use erasers not only as a tool to remove marks, but also to make marks, and if a cheap one will make an interesting smudge, you might find a good use for it. In general, if you want to remove graphite without damaging the paper, the more specialised and expensive erasers are more likely to do the job well.

Kneadable eraser

Kneadable erasers are like Blu-Tack sticky putty. In fact, Blu-Tack makes a good substitute for an artist-quality kneadable eraser, but it can be so efficient that it lifts fibres of the paper as well as the graphite. Art shops sell quality erasers. There are different ones with different tackiness. Again, do experiments with these on your chosen papers. There are many techniques to use this versatile tool. You can form it into a ball, a tear-shape, or snake and dab, roll, drag or rub it. Each makes a unique mark or lifts the graphite in a different way. When the tip gets too dirty, knead and roll it. It's great for making thin fine lines in a light graphite glaze and may be used to draw highlights in hair. For hair-highlights, roll it into a ball, flatten it into a knife-edge and curve it appropriately. Then dab the edge on the paper without dragging it and you will be left with a thin sharp highlight.

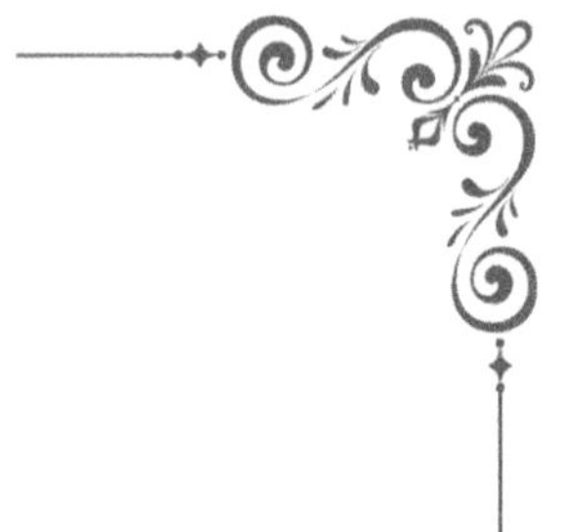

Useful tools

Eraser foil/shield/mask

Art shops and drafting suppliers should stock a thin stainless steel foil which has small shapes cut away. This foil can be used with a conventional eraser to erase small areas without affecting the surrounding graphite.

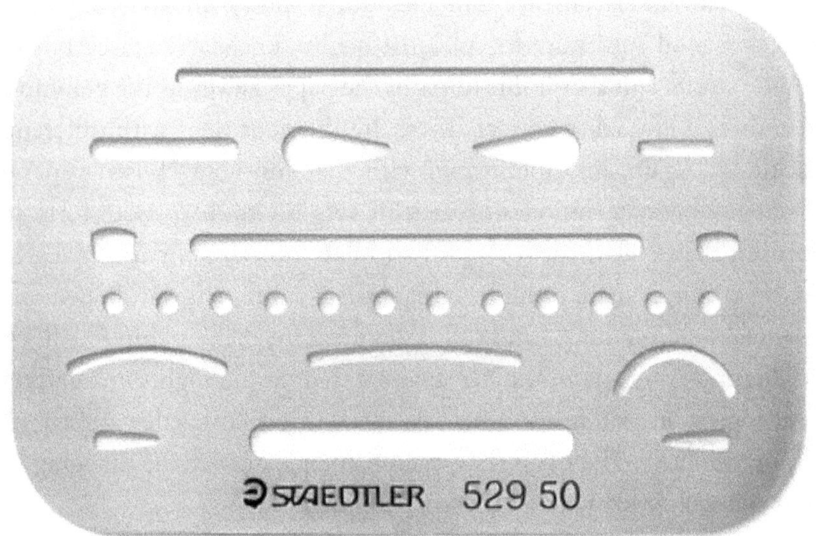

Ruler

What has an artist to do with a ruler! Well, it all comes down to this: You can do it the hard way or the easy way. It's your choice. There is no such thing as cheating in this craft. If you want to produce an accurate rendering of a reference photo or even a live-subject, then why not measure it? If you want to scale the reference up or down, measure it, and use a calculator. With practice, you will get better and find it possible to make remarkably accurate estimates by eye, and sometimes improve on proportion. A photograph often suffers from a lens-distortion and measurement will duplicate this distortion.

If you like to make caricatures or use a loose style to make spontaneous drawings, then there is little need for a ruler. However, the beginner requires success for motivation, and if measuring leads to early feelings of achievement, then do it, and don't feel guilty about it no matter what you hear or read. Eventually, you will rely less on this tool. Pre-photography masters got up to all manner of measuring tricks including grids, pinhole projection and callipers.

Calculator

You might be a good mental calculator, and scaling by two or half should not pose a problem, but what if you wanted to scale a drawing by a factor of 3.7? Use a calculator or a spreadsheet. To use a spreadsheet to scale a column of numbers, put the scale-factor in (say) cell A1. Let's assume there are two numbers in column C2 and C3 to scale by A1. In D2 write the formula =$A$1*C2 then highlight that cell and drag it down into D3 which should give you the formula =$A$1*C3. This method can be extended for many numbers and there will be no arithmetic or keying errors.

Sharpener

I don't recommend a normal pencil sharpener, especially for expensive carbon pencils and softer pencils because it wastes lead. It's much better to use a sharp craft knife. Obviously, for young children and psychopaths, apply the proper amount of supervision.

Emery board

An emery board is a useful tool. It's easy to make one yourself. Find some wet-strength sanding paper. This is the type used by car body repairers. Take a piece of thick card or thin MDF board that you might find in the back of an old cupboard or picture frame. Cut about 5cm x 2cm off the sanding paper to match the size of the board. Use some PVA wood glue to coat the paper and wood. If the wood or cardboard is absorbent you will need to apply another layer of glue after the first application dries. Let it dry till tacky and press the two together. If you like, you can make two or three using various grades of sandpaper. These tools are useful for creating the shapes that you will use for making pencil marks. Keep the resulting dust for use as a mark-making medium.

Knife

A decent craft knife has several uses. The first is to sharpen your wooden pencils. Most of the time, I use mechanical pencils, but the soft and the hard grades are easier to get in wood. The second use is for trimming your paper to size. For this, you will require a flat cutting board and a straightedge. The trick when trimming paper is to put the straightedge over the good portion that you want to keep. If your knife slips away then you only ruin the waste side, and get another go. Use several light strokes rather than one heavy stroke. This is because a heavy stroke will follow imperfections in the cutting board. Several light lines will be accurate. Also—keep a solid and steady pressure on the cutting edge. To do this, make sure that you stand up, and have the cutting edge about waist height.

Finally, with much practice and skill, you can use the craft knife to cut a 45 degree angle-cut in mat board for mounting your pictures in a frame. The process is the same as for a straight cut except this time it might be better to use a glass cutting-board and cut in one heavy stroke. Hold the knife at a 45 degree angle to the mat board, and place the board good side down. You have to cut a little further on the back than the front so the mitres meet. Using glass as a cutting board ensures a clean cut on the face side because of the smooth surface. You can get specialised tools for this which might be worth their value it you use it often but they are expensive. Otherwise, you can get the mat board cut professionally.

Cutting board

A cutting board should be bigger than the work that you are trimming. Typically, plastic, laminate, glass and thick card are good. Don't use wood because it has a grain which will strongly influence your cut. Keep it clean to prevent stains and marks on your stock or finished drawing. Small ridges may develop as it gets used. These may be scraped away using a flat sharp blade on the broad side.

Straightedge

Ideally, you need a flat stainless-steel long straightedge, and a shorter one. The long one will be unwieldy for many small jobs which is why you also need a small one. Choose sizes that are at least as long as the diagonal measurement of the paper that you use. Use a steel straightedge because a plastic ruler will get damaged easily. It's too easy to let the cutting knife ride up onto the plastic and ruin it. Steel is heavier and lies flatter while plastic can more easily lift during a cut.

If it rides up, you will make a bad cut. Wash the steel ruler regularly otherwise it will mark your work because of a build-up of finger-grease and other dirt.

The straightedge is also used for drawing grids or lines on your paper before you start drawing. Some strategically placed guidelines might span the diagonal which is why a straightedge should reach from the top-left corner to bottom right.

If you need a temporary straightedge for drawing (not cutting) and do not have your steel ruler, there are two options. First, you can use a strip of mat board, and second, a piece of paper folded twice. This is thick enough to make a straight line for construction work. Obviously a temporary ruler is not a good cutting guide. However, you can make marks on a paper-ruler for transferring measurements from your reference to the drawing. You can also use it to scale measurements.

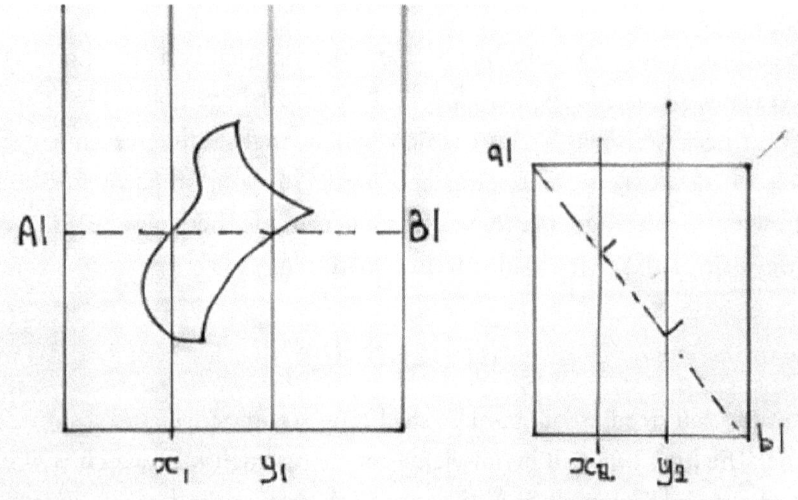

A larger grid can be transformed to a smaller grid using nothing more than folded paper and a pencil. Here is the method: Fold the paper into a ruler-shape. Add some tick marks either at approximate equal spacing, or strategically where there is more detail in the reference. In the example, the paper ruler is laid across the line A1-B1 where the vertical lines on the larger copy are at x1 and y1. Once the tick marks are in place put the improvised ruler onto the smaller copy at an angle a1-b1 so the leftmost and rightmost tick marks line up with the left and right edges of the copy. Now translate these tick marks exactly onto the copy and draw vertical lines at x2 and y2 that cross the tick marks.

Repeat this whole process for the vertical orientation, and the task is complete. This avoids tedious calculation normally used when scaling.

You can do the process in reverse to enlarge a reference.

Value-hole

When you look at a reference, whether this is a live reference or a picture, you automatically look at the whole picture. While this might seem a sensible thing to do, it is not good for training your artistic eye. We work in shades of grey for a graphite picture, and we should pick a piece of grey paper or card that is neutral and about midvalue. Neutral means that it is a grey that is not tinged with colour. When you start to compare grey stock, and even "white" paper, you will discover they are often tinged with colour, but try to find that neutral mid-grey. If you can't, it should be possible to create it with your pencils. Whatever you choose cut a 1cm hole in the middle. This is your value-hole. It is used to mask off all but the part of subject that you find interesting. For example, to study part of a mouth from a photograph, before you use the value-hole, it will look like a typical mouth. It will have two corners, an upper lip, and lower lip. But when you place the value-hole over part of the mouth, it will look like an abstract shape or more likely a few abstract shapes. The previous notion of corner and top-lip are no longer seen. Instead, you will see the real components. You can also compare the value of any abstract shape with the neutral grey of the paper. Let's assume you are trying to draw this sculpture.

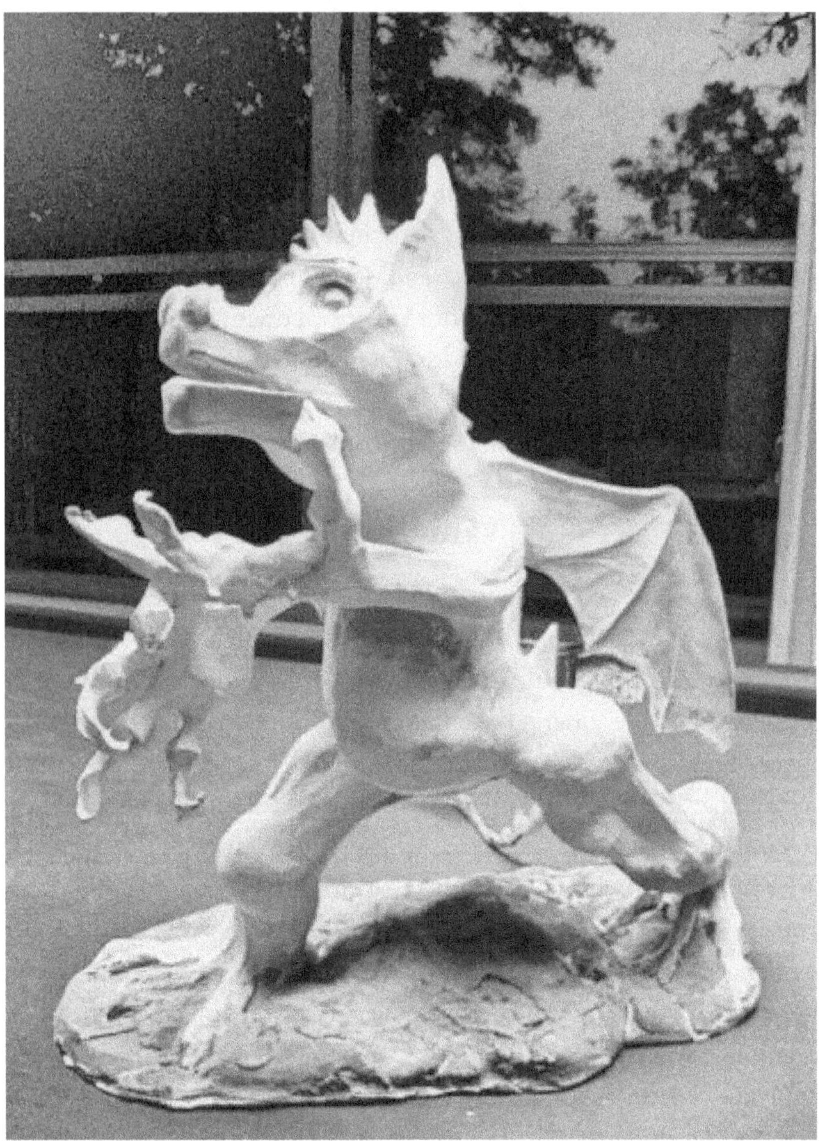

In the next image, I've used several value-holes in a neutral grey mask. Note how much easier it is to read the values. This is because your eye can easily compare the values through the holes with the neutral grey surrounding it.

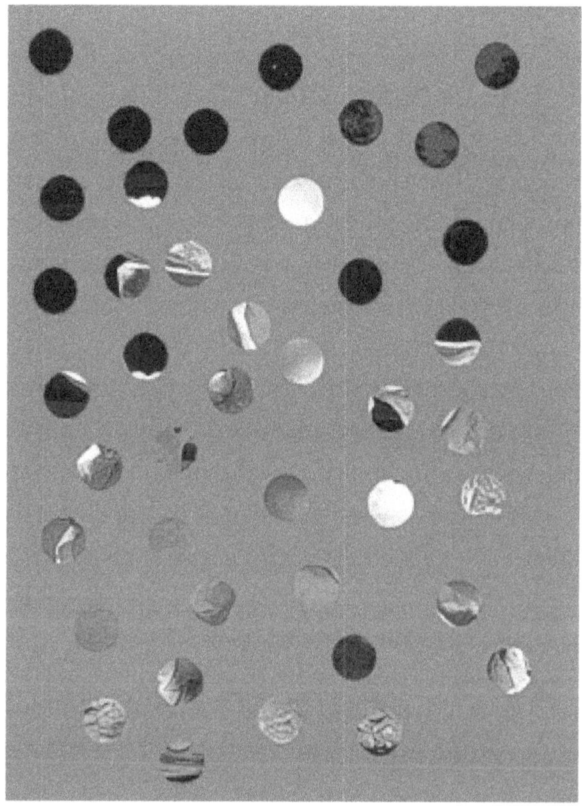

We will mention this again later but it's worth bringing up now: A dark value next to a light value will make the light value look lighter than it really is. You should not ignore this effect.

Use the value-hole frequently to observe your subject. It also works for live subjects if you hold it up in front between your eye and what you observe.

For full-colour references also squint to reduce the strength of colour, and reveal true values.

With practice, you will soon discard the value-hole as your artistic eye becomes more skilled.

Mirror

A mirror has two uses. The first and most obvious is for drawing a self-portrait. There are distinct advantages in doing this. For one, the subject remains available for exactly as long as you wish to draw. For another, the subject never complains unless there are some bipolar issues of course, and finally, the model is always available.

The second use is for judging your work in a new way. You get used to seeing a reference or a live subject from a certain angle. If you change the angle, by turning it upside-down, it looks different, and it makes it easier to compare with your drawing. Using a mirror has an even more dramatic effect. Beginning and experienced artists benefit from viewing both the reference and the drawing as a mirror-image. Sometimes, mirror-image and upside-down helps you to identify abstract shapes.

If you have a computer, and a scanner, it is also possible to flip the image on-screen using a graphics package of some kind.

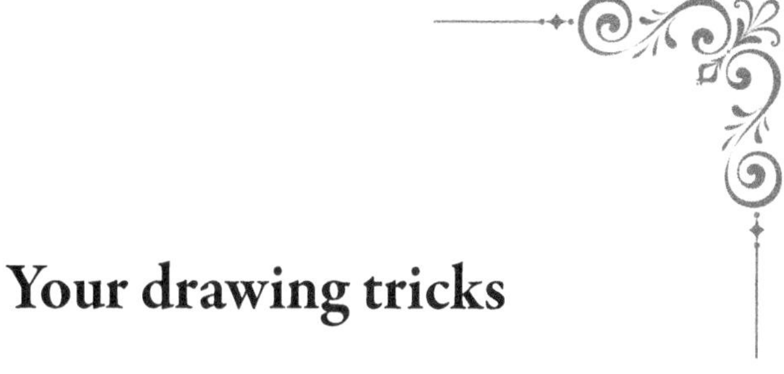

Your drawing tricks

In this chapter, you will find basic elements of drawing. These are standard techniques which you will later combine to produce a good rendering. There are many techniques, and I have given them new names if they are not already known by a common name. To have names for the techniques, allows us to discuss the elements of a finished drawing, or instruct each stage to create a work. An example might be: "Print a reference. Choose a tooth. Locate strategic lines. Transfer the outline. Sketch in the darks, lift the highlights, apply under skin-texture, layer with 2B circularism..." At this stage, this might not mean much, but please read on or use the contents and search-tool to find out what this all means.

Choosing tooth.

As discussed, the paper that you choose will profoundly affect the end-result. A rough tooth will take darks well. It will be difficult to create fine details, but easy to simulate certain textures. Your choice will depend on the feel, depth and subject matter. Some subjects benefit from a rough grainy image, while others look better on smooth paper with fine details. It is your choice as the artist to decide how you would like to present the scene. A smoky nightclub scene could be drawn on rough paper to simulate subdued tones and detail as you would expect in dim light. You could also approach this by using a smooth paper and draw with graphite-dust. You could use rough paper, and selectively burnish parts of the paper. Here, the goal is to use the paper's tooth for dramatic effect but burnish the paper where you need to put fine detail.

Here is a description of how tooth affects your drawing, and how you can control the result by knowing what is happening to the paper and pencil as you draw. The shape of the tip of the pencil is important. Let's define a few shapes.

1. Smooth point
2. Smooth wedge
3. Sharp wedge
4. Sharp cylinder
5. Sharp point
6. Broad flat smooth
7. Broad flat sharp

Each of these behaves differently on paper with varying tooth and pencil grade. Of course, as you rub the pencil point on the paper it changes shape. When you work, try to imagine which shape the tip is becoming. For example, a Smooth point can easily wear into a sharp wedge or a smooth wedge depending on how you use it.

Graphite flake size and tooth size.

Let's review: Soft pencils have more graphite than clay. Clay has dull small hard particles while graphite has larger flat shiny flakes. Softer pencils have even bigger flakes. Therefore, the success of trying to fill the valleys in the tooth of the paper depends on the choice of pencil grade and the choice of paper. This is an important concept, and when you do enough experimentation with various papers and pencils, you will gain more control over the result. The shape of the pencil tip also affects how the graphite and clay particles sit in the valleys or on the peaks.

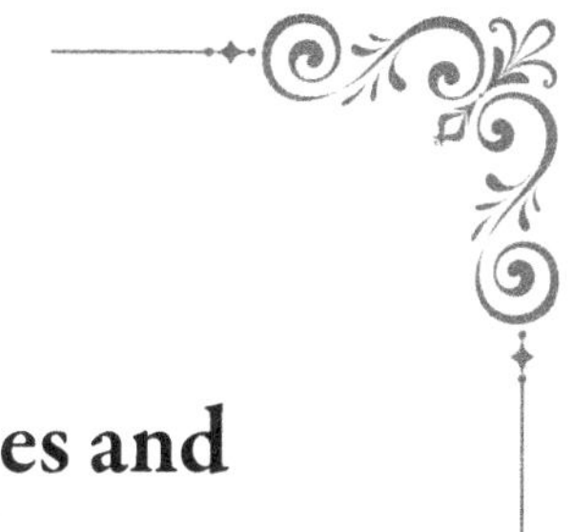

Pencil point shapes and their uses

Smooth point

The smooth point may be used to shade an area in layers without crushing the tooth. With a smooth point, you can cover an area without showing pencil lines. It is used for general gradual shading without indicating texture.

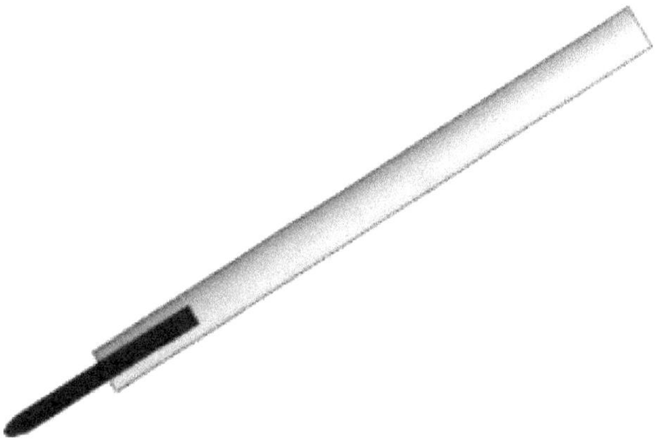

Texture may be added by using pencils of different grades in varying patterns in several layers. With this technique, you can avoid blending. A hard pencil with a smooth point used as a glaze over a finished area will help to unify the drawing. This adds realism by ensuring the paper is fully covered.

Smooth wedge

A smooth wedge shape can be used very much like the smooth point. However, since it makes a wider stroke, it will coat the peaks of the tooth, leaving the valleys.

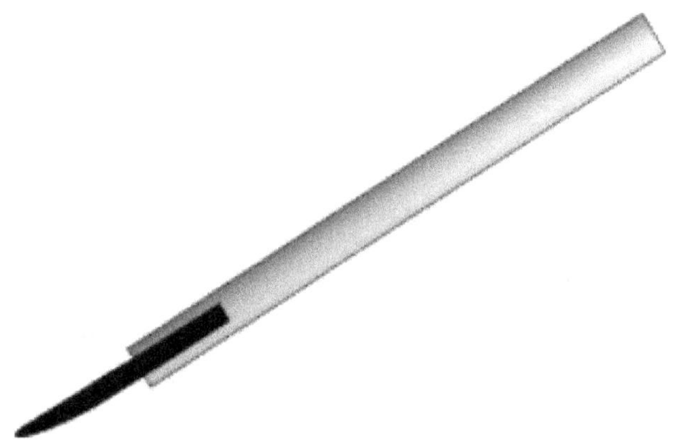

When you are using a layering technique, you can use a sharp or blunt point to draw lines followed by a smooth wedge in a different pencil grade. The sharp point can fill the valleys better, while a different grade can coat the peaks. (See the section on graphite flake size and tooth size). If the size of the graphite flake is greater than the distance between the peaks of the paper's tooth, these flakes will sit on top and across the tops. A later application with a hard sharp point can push these flakes deeper into the paper. Soft pencil on a fine-tooth with light pressure can give a grainy effect. This might be the look you want, or it could be only one step in finding a suitable texture.

Sharp Wedge

The sharp wedge is versatile. If you hold it flat and accurately against the paper, gentle application can give a smooth even finish. At the same time, slightly turning it clockwise or anticlockwise gives you a long sharp edge which you can use to drag a definite mark downwards. If you only slightly twist it, you can get a sharp edge on one side, and a graduated application to the other.

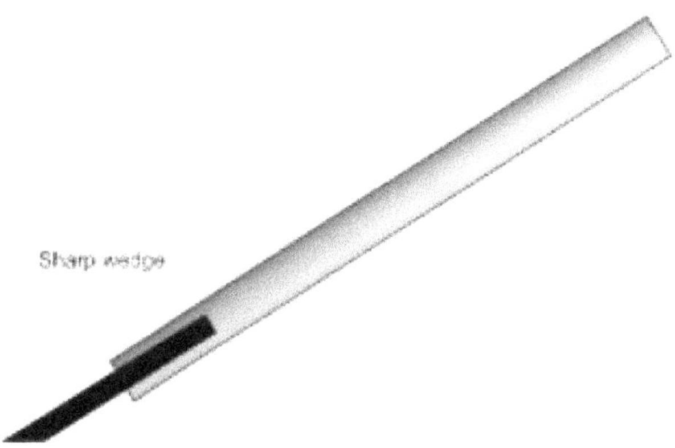

Alternatively, the far point of the wedge becomes sharp, so you can raise the pencil perpendicular to the paper and get deep into the valleys of the tooth in the paper. I've used a sharp wedge like this many times to create texture. It's handy because alternate use of a perpendicular and flat tip hones the tip continuously.

Sharp cylinder

This is useful for making fine marks. To prepare the pencil point is easy. You need an emery board or fine sandpaper. Hold the pencil perpendicular to the emery board and make a short even stroke. This will quickly prepare the pencil point as a cylinder.

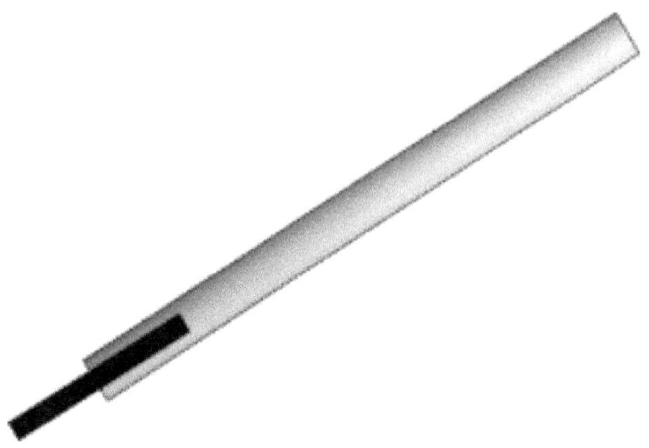

It works best with mechanical pencils because the lead is uniform. The cylinder has a sharp edge all the way around its circumference and you can use it sector by sector. Turn the pencil as you use it to get a fresh edge. Or you can gradually let it wear into a hard or soft wedge. This technique is good for simulating texture. If you make a circular mark, the pencil line thickness will graduate from broad to fine to broad. Compare this with the Sharp point.

Sharp point—Wooden pencil

If using a wooden pencil, remove a lot of wood to expose about 2 cm of lead. This seems like a very long tip but it lets you to see your work properly without being obscured by the tool, and reduces a need to stop and cut away more wood.

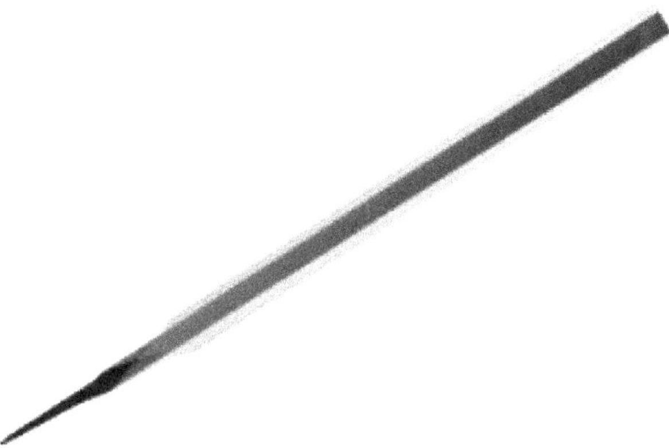

Shape it with a knife and the emery board. If using a mechanical pencil, use the emery board to create a sharp point.

Sharp point—Mechanical pencil

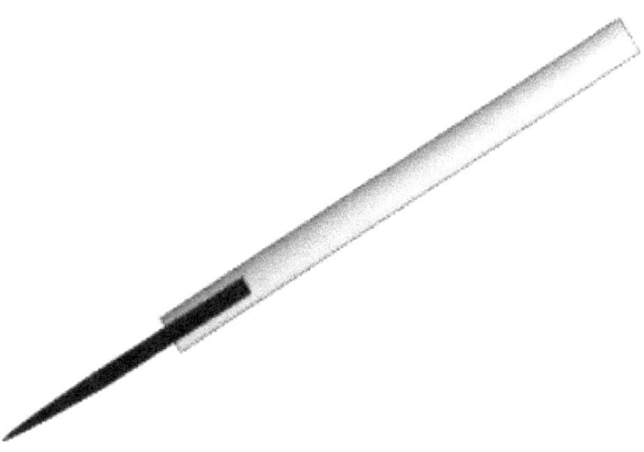

When you make a circular mark with a sharp point the width will be a reasonably consistent. It wears quickly into a sharp cylinder or smooth point if you vary the angle continuously. The sharp point is good for fine detail like the patterns in the eye. It pushes graphite deep into the tooth of the paper.

Broad flat smooth tip

This is the shape the pencil tends to wear into as you use it. It's handy for rendering smooth tones and layers without texture. Use it gently on the paper to avoid crushing the tooth.

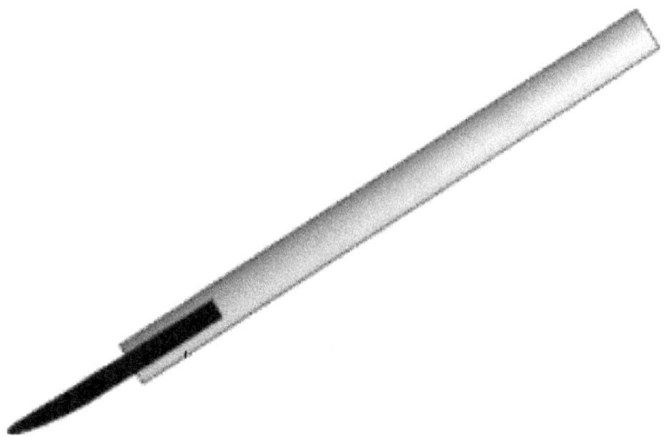

A light application will only deposit graphite on the tops of the tooth. If you would like to push the graphite into the paper deeper, a second layer with a sharp hard pencil point will do this. Alternatively, a small paintbrush or any of the blending tools will give various results.

Broad flat sharp tip

If you hold the pencil at a shallow angle accurately without twisting it, it will eventually form a broad flat sharp point. At this stage, it will smoothly render large areas without leaving definite marks. Once honed, use the sharp side in one fluid movement to occasionally making a light or more definite mark. This helps to bring realism to your drawings by simulating small flaws and texture.

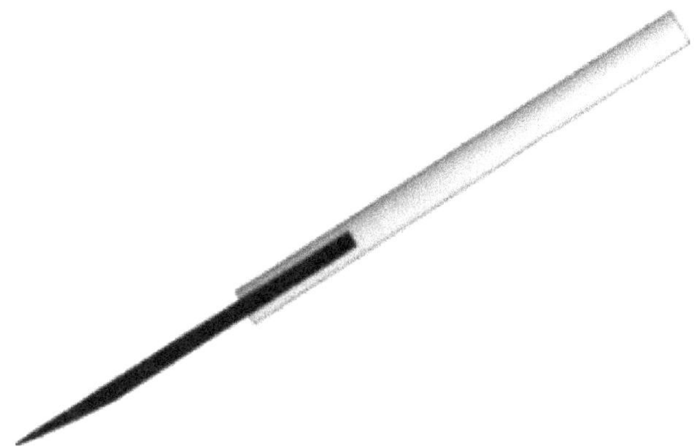

You can also use the emery board to make this shape.

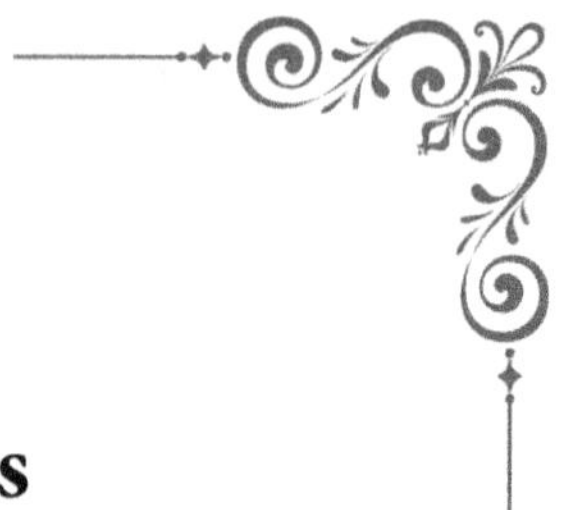

Blending tools

Blending will move the graphite around on the paper. It spreads and pushes it into the tooth. It also has the potential to change the characteristics of the paper by bending or crushing the tooth. It's not usually desirable to crush the tooth, but occasionally, and in moderation it will create an effect that you can use.

There are many items that you can use for blending, and because of their individual characteristics, the results vary. Effects will, of course also vary depending on the paper, and the grade of pencil that you have used. Blending softens detail, smears edges, smooths transitions, and prepares the paper for the next layer. You might like to consider gentle blending in shadow areas because by not crushing the tooth too much, and by pushing graphite into the tooth, the next light application of graphite will make it darker. An application-blend-application sequence might need to be done up to 14 times before the paper is fully saturated. If, after all this application, the tooth is still relatively undamaged, the dark area will not shine much. As mentioned, a lack of shine is required for shadows. Also, the lack of detail that blending causes is suitable for shadows.

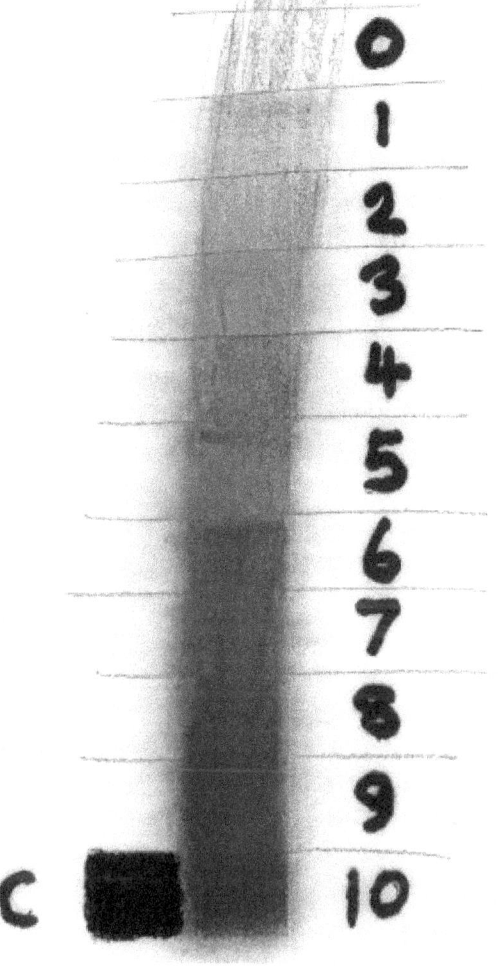

In the illustration, I blended a 2B mechanical pencil applied with a broad smooth point. See in level 0 how the graphite sits on top of the paper's tooth. Level 1 is one application of blending with a paintbrush. The graphite has been moved into the valleys. This process has been repeated up to level 10 when the paper is almost totally saturated with 2B grade pencil. The mark labelled C is one application of "USA General's Carbon Sketch (TM) No 595 Soft". It is simply not possible to get a graphite pencil as black and non-shiny as this but the correct application of blending and gentle application allows you to push the graphite to its limit without crushing the tooth. Note how the blended result is devoid of pencil marks.

In lighter areas like the skin on a person's cheek, a realistic drawing will show skin pores and little blemishes. Blending will not allow such detail, so we resort to different techniques like circularism for creating detailed but smooth transitions. However, it can be an advantage to blend the first layer because this will produce a smooth surface. This smooth surface can make the application of detail easier to control and more subtle. It is surprising how small a tonal variation can produce the impression of a little pimple or dent in skin.

Here is a list of blending tools that you should use in experiments. It's not practical to list all the characteristics here because it depends on many variables like the particular paper you are using, the quality and grade of the pencils, and the pressure you use when blending.

- Chamois leather
- Paper stump or tortillon
- Tissue
- Small brush
- Finger
- Rag

There is one major technique to try. Most people might make a blend-stroke one way, stop, and then reverse without lifting the tool. This will sometimes cause a dark spot where you stopped and changed direction. It's most likely better to blend in a continuous motion without lifting or stopping or in one direction only. Here are three techniques using a paper tortillon over one application of 2B mechanical pencil.

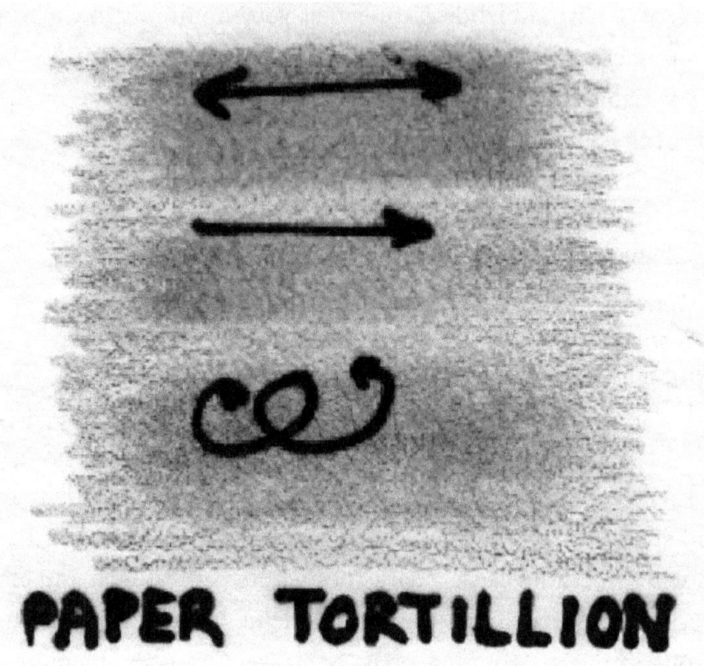

The top blend is made using a back and forth sweep in the same direction as the pencil marks. The middle illustration is from a repeated left-to-right stroke. The bottom one is from continuous circular motion. The effects are subtle but important as realistic portrait drawing is a very precise art. Particularly in the midvalues, the tiniest variation in value can make or break a likeness or profoundly affect realism. Luckily, there are only a few operations to use in pencil portraits that cannot be undone.

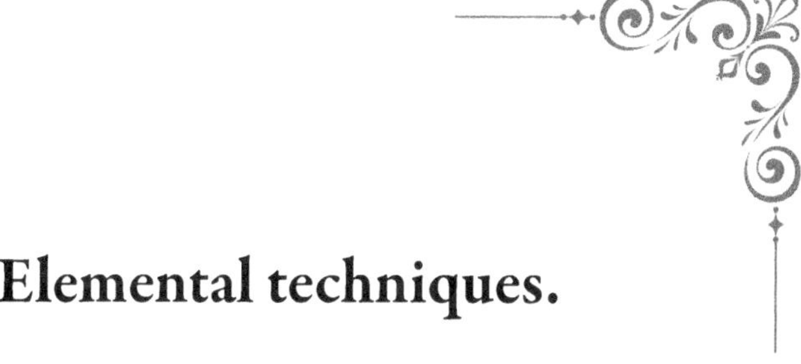

Elemental techniques.

In this chapter, you will find detailed descriptions on various techniques for laying out and rendering your drawing.

How to hold a pencil.

Many people were taught how to hold a pencil in the first few days of school. I was taught to let my hand drop in a relaxed state, lay the pencil on my middle finger, and grip it between thumb and forefinger, near to the point, just before the wood slopes away. This is fine for writing but nearly useless for drawing. I've seen many people who were never taught at all and hold a pencil almost in a fist. I find it extraordinary how they manage to control it. For drawing, there are better ways to hold the pencil.

Tight grip

I don't recommend this unless you are concentrating on a definite line in a small area, like perhaps a line inside the iris of an eye. On small drawings, I've used this technique with a powerful magnifying glass in selected areas. A tight grip restricts movement, and all control comes from the muscles in the fingers. This ruins fluidity for longer marks and hampers control of pressure. Try to use a grip which will allow movement to come from the shoulder down. This is most important for large sweeping marks.

Light grip

When you hold the pencil lightly, you get more control over the marks that you make because the movement can come from larger muscles in your arm. A light grip also gives more control over pressure. In general, repeated applications of light pressure give a better result than a single heavy mark. But there are times when a single heavy mark is very successful

End grip

It is natural to hold the pencil near the tip for writing, and fine work. For drawing and rendering, it is useful to hold the pencil right at the end in a loose grip so the only marks made on the paper are from the weight of the pencil itself. Sometimes you will hardly see a mark, and be tempted to add pressure, but repeated marks and layers will gradually shade the area. This technique lets you render a drawing without blending, and simultaneously retains texture. With this pencil-hold, the pencil makes a shallow contact with the paper, and therefore a broad mark.

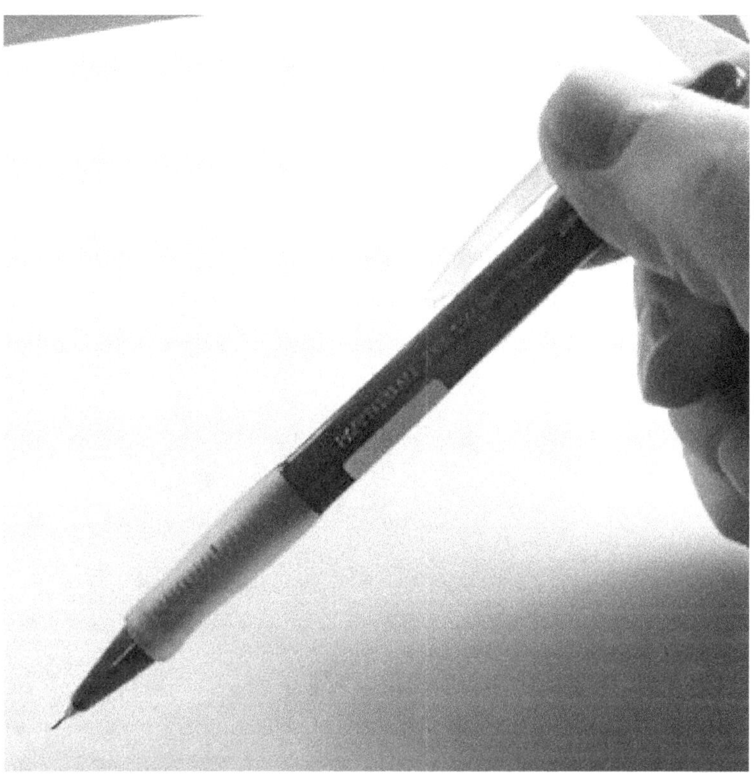

This end grip is the most useful technique for creating subtle midvalues and skin texture.

Vertical

If you hold the pencil mid-way, in a three-fingered grip and reasonably tight, you can still use the major muscles of the arm to make a mark. The marks made while the pencil is held this way will vary depending on the shape of the pencil tip. A round sharp tip will penetrate the tooth of the paper and make a consistent and sharp mark as you pull it through an arc. A blunt wedge will make an arc that varies in thickness as you move through the arc. Experiment with different pencil tips and grades to see what effects you can get.

Near perpendicular

A pencil held a little off vertical will make a sharp mark with most pencil-tip shapes. Compare this with the acute angle.

Acute

When you hold the pencil at a shallow angle to the page, a softer broader mark is made. As the pencil wears, the mark gets wider. Compare this with the results you get with a near perpendicular hold.

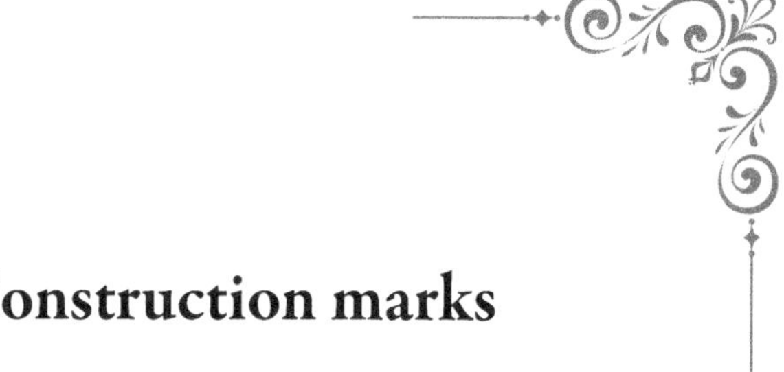

Construction marks

Measured marks

A measured mark is one that you place on the page at a position dependent on a physical comparison with the reference, and using a measuring tool like a stick or ruler. It is usually a light dot or short mark which will later become part of the drawing or erased if required.

Construction lines

Construction lines are lines which are not part of your final drawing. Rarely, the artist may decide to leave some construction lines visible as sometimes they have an artistic merit. This of course depends on the type of drawing that you wish to produce. Since we are concentrating on rendering the most realistic portraits that we can manage, it's most likely that you will erase or draw over all construction marks. The construction mark is made very light with a soft pencil. This makes it easy to remove. They can be made freehand, with a ruler or compass.

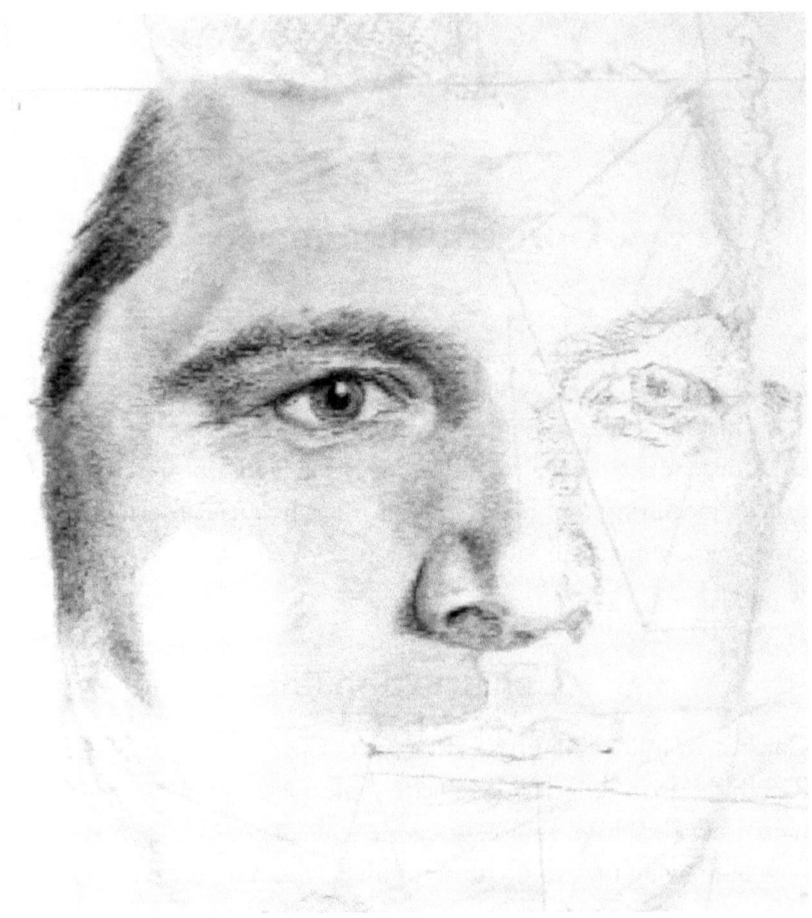

The work in progress above clearly shows some construction marks that I call strategic lines. These are the lines that bound features on the face. Many people use a grid but I find that too mechanical. These lines are made by dragging a soft mechanical pencil using an end-grip. Don't use more pressure than the weight of the pencil, and don't use a hard grade or you will not be able to remove the construction lines.

Margins and tick marks

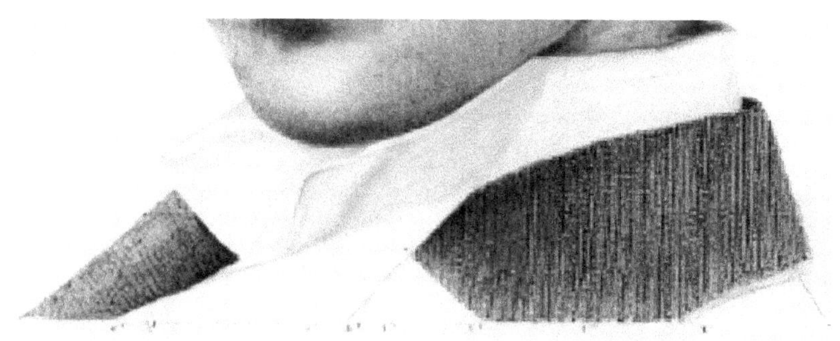

Don't draw right to the edge of the paper for two reasons. First—it makes it hard to mount in a frame. You need a margin for the mount board. Second—it gives you a space to make little tick-marks and references for strategic lines. Sometimes I make dozens of strategic lines and labelling them helps to identify which ones I am looking at.

Sketch marks

Make sketch marks with a medium-soft pencil grade B will do. Use it light and loose. This is a preliminary stage before proper rendering. You need to build on the marks, cover them, lighten them or erase them as you go. The main goal of these sketch marks is to get the contour, proportions, and rough values in place. Once you are satisfied with that, then fine rendering can begin. Here is the early stage of a small drawing before rendering over the sketch marks.

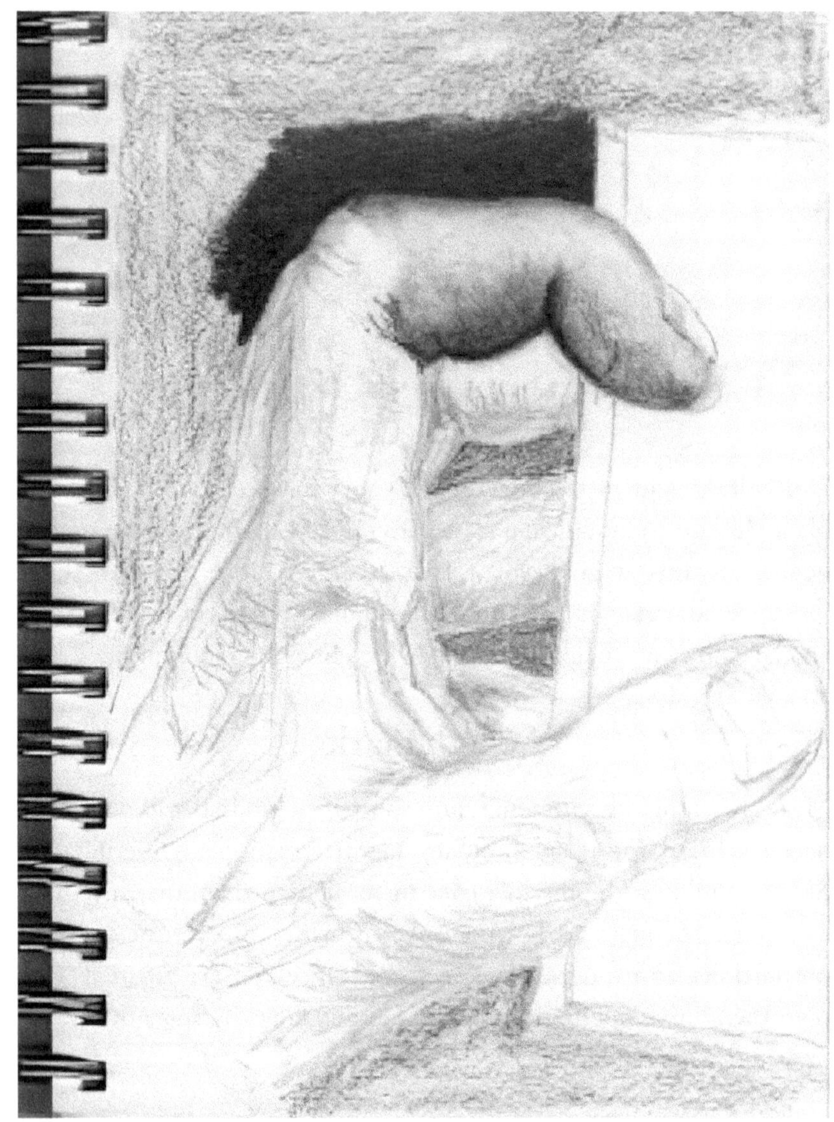

Transfer methods

Whether your reference material is a physical object or a photograph, you will use a method to transfer the image to paper. This important step establishes contour and proportion. If you draw from life, then the subject—a person—is sitting in front of you. Your options are not limited to the method of "by eye". Endless debate can be found arguing the merits of various methods of transfer. Don't get too involved with these arguments. Even the old masters used whatever tools they could invent or find to make copying easier and faster. The real skill is involved with composition, rendering and the way that marks are used on the paper.

Transfer by eye

This means that you don't use any method of judging proportion and space other than looking at the subject and reproducing what you see (no rulers). It can be very successful, but the beginner and intermediate artist will find this challenging. However, it is a good exercise. It is a good idea to try this often. Let's run through a scenario where you want to draw someone's portrait live, by eye.

First, find the approximate middle of the page, top to bottom. This is the eye-line most comfortable for a portrait. Draw a horizontal and a vertical line. Where they cross will be the middle point between the eyes. Estimate the size and shape of one eye, and lightly draw an oval which centres on the cross. This is your reference. The distance between someone's eyes is about the width of their eye. Now you can draw the left and right eye by duplicating this oval. Now draw a circular construction line around each eye. This will remind you that an eye is a ball and therefore the folds over the eyelids and under the eyes are influenced by this shape. Additionally, the bony eye socket is a rather large hole and the skin falls differently in this area. Older people have less elasticity in their skin, so in this area it tends to sag more and show fine wrinkles.

Drop two vertical lines from the inside corner of each eye. The width of the nose is approximately the same. Most noses flare a little wider than this reference, and some noses are narrower. It's these small differences which make us individuals, and these are the differences that you need to identify to get a likeness.

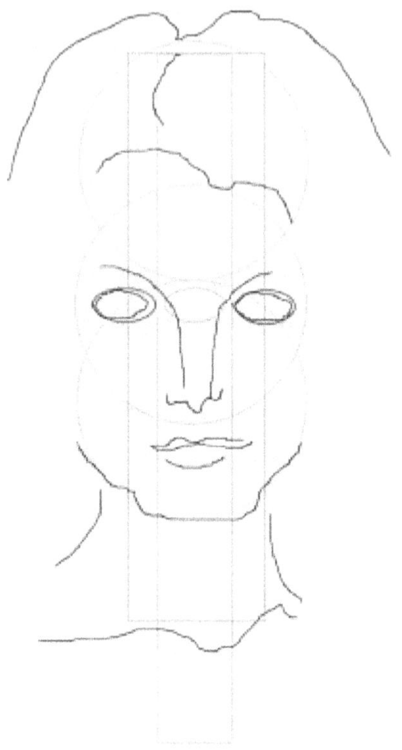

Now you need to establish a vertical reference. This is more difficult since you have already picked a horizontal reference as the two must be in proportion. Look at your subject and imagine a perfect circle about the centre point so the circumference of the circle touches just outside the corners of the eyes. Another circle, of the same size passes through the pupils. One more sits on top of that. Draw two vertical lines through the pupils.

This establishes most of the rough positions and proportions for a face. Note that eyes are about half way between the top of the head, and the bottom of the chin. Not shown are the ears. These vary, but often extend from eyebrows to the bottom of the nose. The mouth is about as wide as the distance between pupils. The neck appears under the chin a little wider than the edges of the mouth.

When many people draw a face, they don't notice the large distance from the eyes to the top of the head. Children almost always draw the eyes right on the top of the head. This is because we are accustomed from birth to focus on someone's eyes and mouth.

The circles-method just discussed is only one way to view the proportions of a face. Some other methods are based on boxes, and spheres, and others on lines around a single sphere that are a little like lines of longitude and latitude. Further study will reveal theories about the golden mean, the rule of thirds.

Some experts encourage artists to learn the bone structure and muscle structure in fine detail. I think it is a good idea to have a reasonable appreciation of the muscle and bone structure. For this, you should consult an anatomy book. As a teaser, please study this 17th century drawing of the human skull from a Dutch anatomy textbook. (Public domain image)

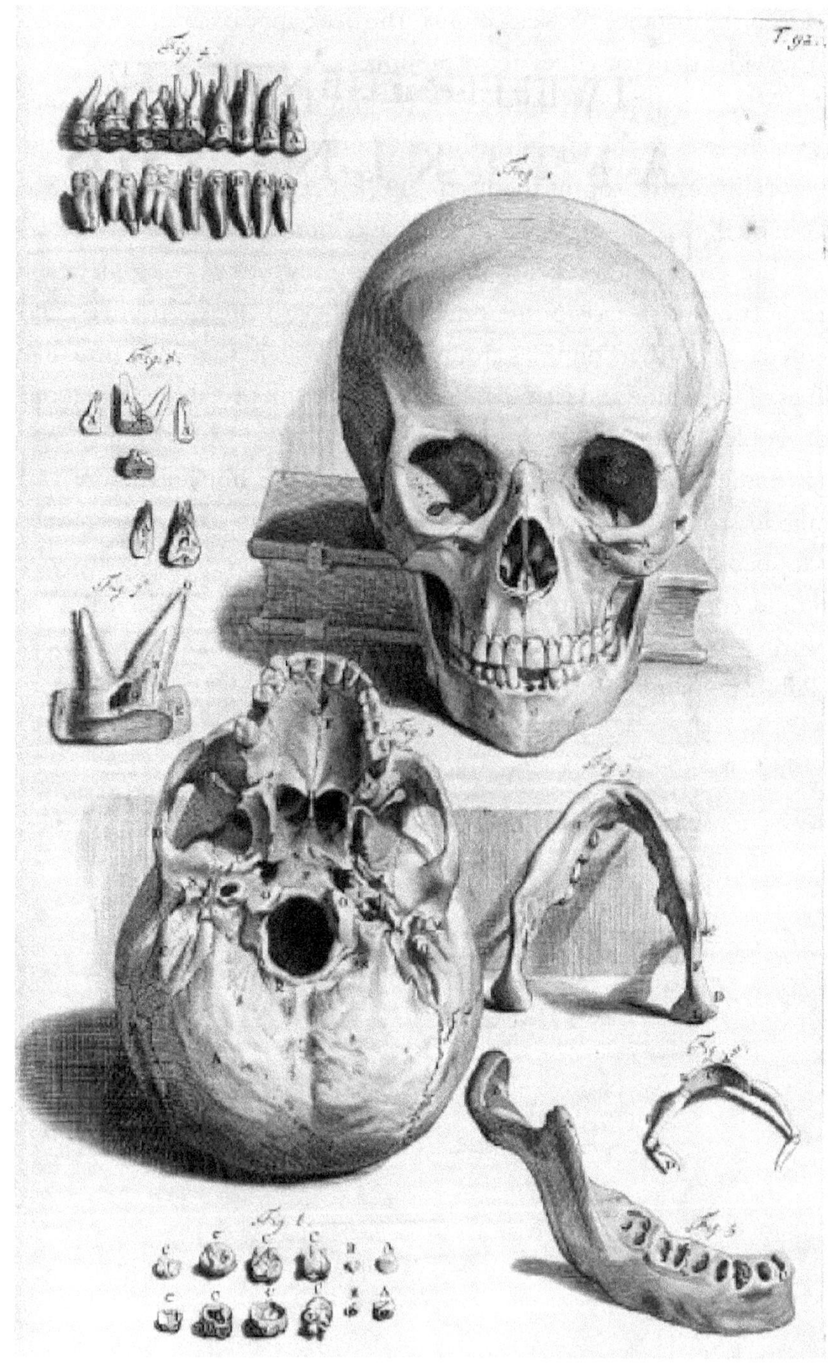

You need to practice careful observation. Continuously perform a comparative mental measurement between various features. An internal mental commentary might run like this: "His nose seems to be about as long as the smile is wide... His nostrils are flared, and I can drop two lines down from the centre of his pupils to guide me. The top of his ears are almost as high as his eyebrows. If I imagine a straight line along the angled jaw line, it extends to just cut the lower part of his earlobe and the bottom of his ear lines up with the bottom of his nose..."

You need to make these comparative observations often, and reproduce the relationships on your drawing. Remember the face is not a solid object. Even ignoring the effect of muscles, the shape of the face depends on other things like gravity or strong wind. When someone tilts his or her head to one side, the cheek is pulled down by gravity. If you don't take these things into account, the picture will look false.

Measurement by ruler

From a live subject or paper reference, you can use a ruler to measure the relationships between various features. Finding and laying out the initial proportions is crucial for likeness and it is worth finding *any* method that works to get this done. There is plenty more work to do when the proportions and contour are set. Artists who do portraiture for a living need the fastest method possible to get the proportions into sketch form. Even those who are good at free-sketching without tools might use a projector or other methods to save time. Many serious portrait artists use a calliper, and stone-sculptors use a pointing machine to move the measurements from a clay model to the final artwork. Today, even lasers are used as measuring tools.

Transfer by permanent marker.

This is a technique that I found by accident. Normal copy paper is absorbent, so if you print a picture using normal copy paper, it can serve as a reference in the following way: Draw on the picture-side using a permanent marker—the ink bleeds through to the other side. Scan the reverse side into a computer and flip the image. Here is the sequence in pictures.

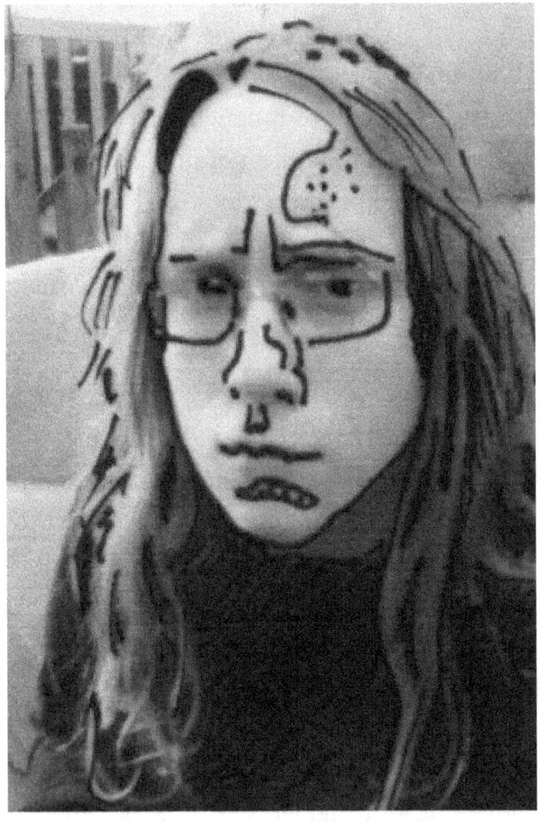

Print the picture on copy paper. Use a fine-tip permanent marker to draw over key features. Just find the minimum number of contours that gives a likeness. Turn the paper over.

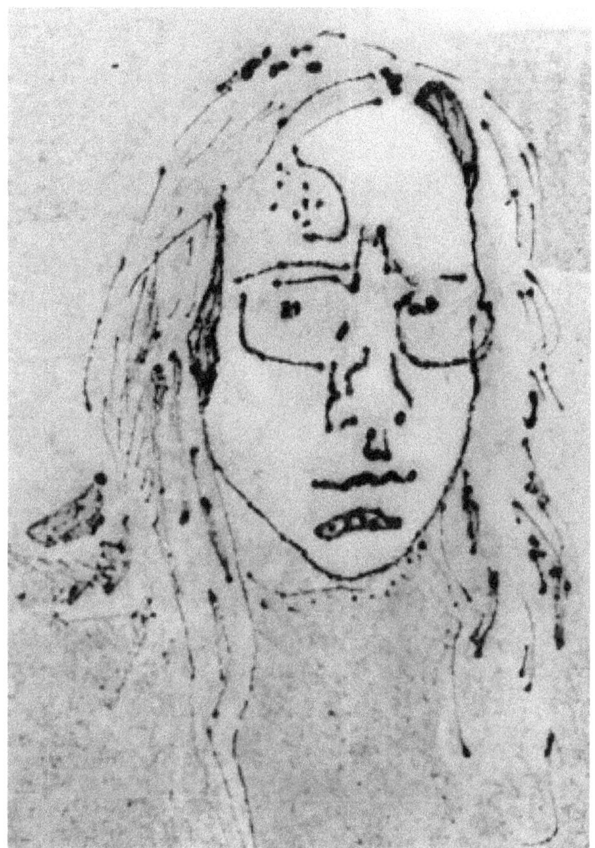

Scan this back into the computer, flip it horizontally, adjust the contrast to expose only the contour lines and print this out.

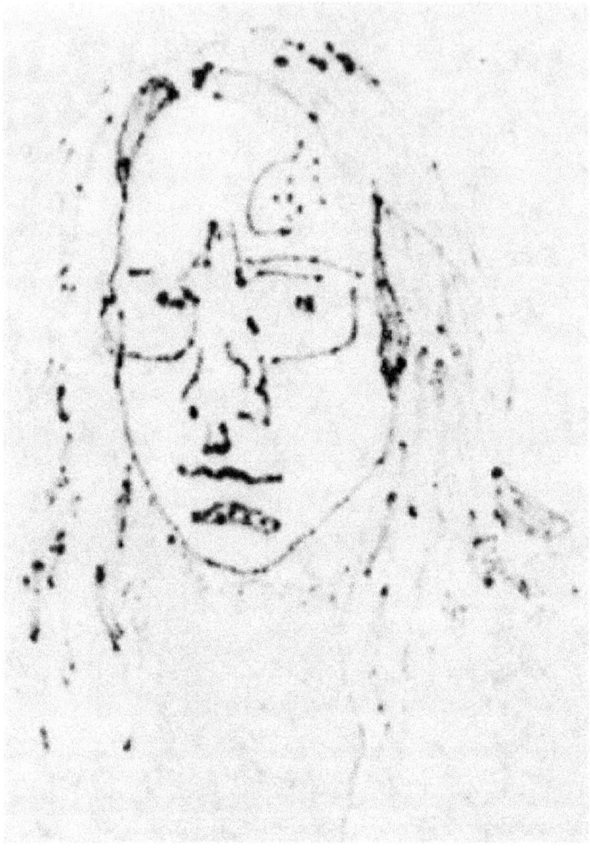

This method quickly isolates the important contours from parts of the original photograph that might otherwise distract. Use one of the following suggestions and transfer these lines to your final drawing paper.

Transfer by grid

The grid method is popular. Many graphite and portrait artists using other mediums will use a grid. Often, there is a photographic reference available. A grid is laid over the top of this in one of at least three ways.

Draw

You can simply draw over the reference. This of course ruins the photograph or other reference but it is simple and effective. One disadvantage is how lines eventually start to confuse because they interfere with the interpretation of the reference. Remember: photographs have inherent problems with focus and distortion. Sometimes you need to adjust these, and a permanent grid on the reference can get in the way. Here is a grid drawn over a printed contour guide that was produced using the marker method.

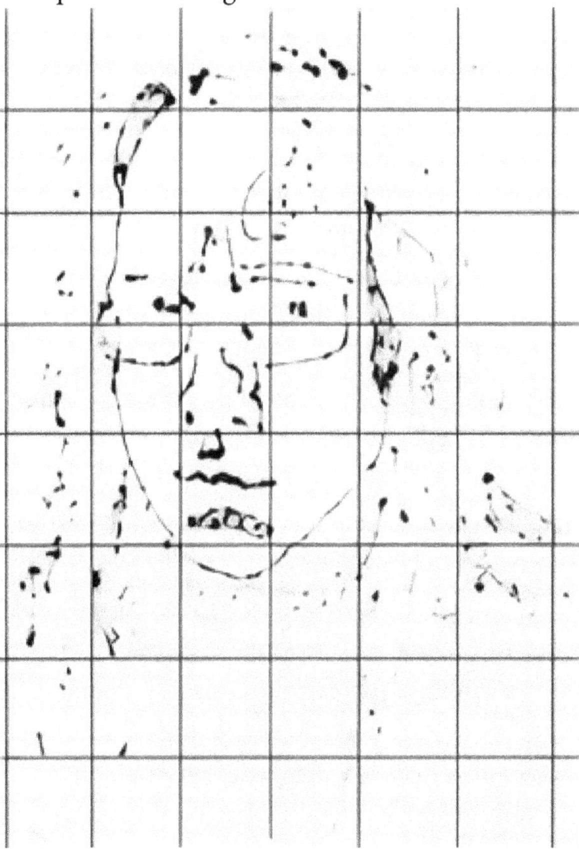

Overlay

An acetate sheet prepared with a grid can be used to overlay a grid. This has the advantages of being reusable and removable, and of course does not damage the reference. It's important to find some way to fix it to the reference to prevent it moving. A slight disadvantage is that the grid is set and you may need a new one for another drawing depending on the size.

Print a grid

You can prepare a digital reference with grid-lines using a computer then print it. It's also useful to convert the image to grey-scale before printing. This helps you judge value without added confusion from colour. Printout-quality will not equal the original—especially if you had to first use a scanner to digitise the image. Therefore, also refer to the original while working on the drawing.

A grid should be prepared lightly on your blank paper. Use a 2B 0.5mm mechanical pencil. Hold it right at the end and let just the weight of the pencil rest on the paper. Drag the pencil along the ruler to make a light mark without crushing the paper.

The source grid and the target grid can be different scales. You can use a smaller grid on your drawing to shrink the image, and a larger one to expand the image. If you shrink it too much, it becomes a challenge to apply all the lovely detail that you see in the original. But expanding too much will leave you wanting more detail in the original. When shrinking, you can either miss out detail or use a sharp pencil, a magnifying glass, and a steady hand. When expanding, you can either accept that your drawing will look best from a reasonable distance, or invent imaginary details. The latter can, with practice, lead to a hyperrealistic rendering.

There is no rule that forces you to use the same scale in both the x and the y axes. An increase in the y-axis scale will make your drawing elongated, and an increase in the x-axis scale will make it squashed. This might be an effect that you want. It is also possible to map your reference to a grid that varies in scale along the x and y axes. In this case, you can render a normal front-on reference to a drawing that appears to lie down on a flat paper.

Transfer by Strategic lines

"Strategic lines" is a technique that I invented because I don't like the clinical dimensions of a grid to be forced on the drawing. Strategic lines are like a grid gone crazy. The lines do not need to be strictly horizontal and vertical. There are more lines where there exists more detail and fewer lines where it doesn't matter. A prominent angle in the reference suggests a good place to put a line. Most lines span the whole page at an angle, and sometimes, where these lines cross inside the reference, it makes sense to start a new line.

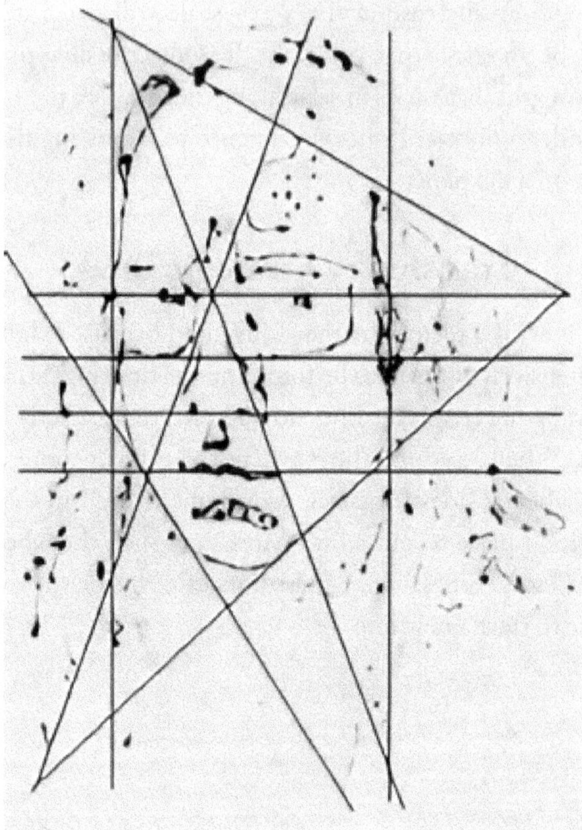

If you choose the lines well, it becomes easier to see contours and boundaries. You can almost imagine the contours before laying down any graphite because often, the main features are bounded by Strategic lines.

I advocate this method over the grid method because it frees up your creativity. I think the grid method is too controlling. When you use the Strategic lines method often, it becomes much easier to do it from life and without clinical measurement. This method helps you to develop an artistic eye.

Transfer by flipbook method

The flip book method uses a reference placed over the drawing. Then you flip it on and off by curling it from one corner to find out where to place marks. There is no grid to mark, and no preparation involved.

At least for a flexible reference, the flip book method seems like a good idea but it has problems. It can only be used for one-to-one scaling. The reference can get damaged by constant curling, and it's surprisingly difficult to place a mark in the right place. It needs to be firmly fixed at one end to the drawing, or repeatedly realigned.

Transfer by light-box

A light box is a successful tool for copying. It will help the beginner greatly. This is little more than a sheet of glass under which a light shines. Of course, it can be made more useful by using a strip fluorescent light and with a foot-switch for turning it on and off. You place the reference on the glass, then your copy-paper over the top. When the light is flicked on, much of the detail, and the major features of the reference are visible. From there, you simply trace the original. In my opinion, beginners, and advanced artists may use this method for two different reasons. The beginner will benefit from early success, while the advanced artist stands to save a lot of time. The intermediate artist should not use this crutch exclusively, and in fact should increasingly experiment with free-hand drawing. Otherwise, it is hard to progress. Like the grid, a light box tends to encourage rather clinical results. Once you get more experienced, it becomes possible to break away from the tightness. Of course, it is only useful for 1:1 transfer.

Transfer by tracing

The tracing method is an obvious technique. You obtain some thin translucent paper, lay it over the original, and draw lines to coincide with outline and boundaries of shapes. Then you scribble over the back of the tracing paper with soft pencil, place it onto your copy-paper and draw over all the lines again. The pressure through the tracing paper transfers graphite from its rear onto your copy paper.

I don't like this method for four reasons:

• Tracing twice introduces accumulative errors, and these errors are mechanical and uncontrolled. It's not as if the deviations have artistic merit which benefits the drawing.

• It's too clinical for my liking.

• The method makes a one-to-one copy with no chance to scale the result.

• Worst: the pressure of tracing often embosses the copy paper which leaves an awkward impression to work around or disguise.

You should try it even if it is only to compare results with other methods.

Transfer by projection

Projection seems a little like tracing. But in this case, you can scale the reference, and there is only one step from reference to copy. Some advanced artists make use of projectors. They save time, and perhaps most striking, is how you can use them to scale to wall-sized images. One annoying disadvantage is how your arm casts a shadow over the copy as you work, but that's a small price to pay for the speed. Commercial projectors are available for this purpose. You could use a standard (and now dated) overhead projector where the reference is transferred to acetate using a photocopier or computer. You could scan the original or photograph it to get it into a digital format. Obviously, this is a studio-only device. It's hardly practical to draw outdoors, on a train or in a coffee-shop when using a projector. They are expensive, so this method seems to be targeted at the professional or advanced and keen amateur.

Transfer by transforming onto a curved surface

A grid, tracing and other similar methods copy one-to-one which means the scale of the original matches exactly the scale of the copy. A projector potentially scales up or down linearly which means the relative proportions are not altered. Other transformations are possible which will deliberately distort the copy compared with the original. The simplest technique is to scale the x and the y axes differently. This squashes or stretches the copy but the transformation is still made from the reference to a flat surface. Now we ask what would happen if we wanted to transform the reference onto a curved surface. In this case, you have to use two different coordinate systems. Imagine looking into a shiny kettle. Your nose would be closest and due to the curve of the kettle it will appear larger compared with your other features. Now imagine a flat grid reflected in this kettle. Its lines would bend. See the picture below for an example of a transformation to a curved surface. If we set up a curved target grid, use the grid method to transfer the image.

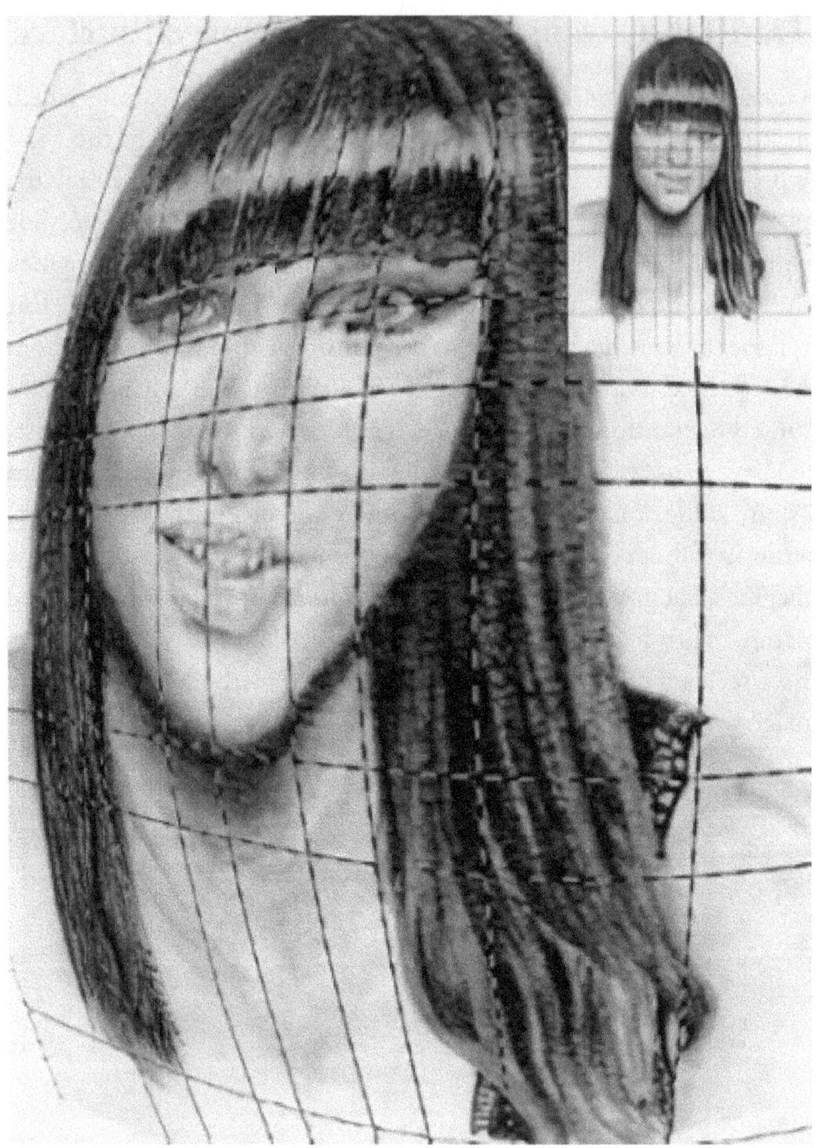

In this example, a grid was placed on the reference, and then the grid was reproduced as if on a curved surface on the target copy. Then the image was transferred exactly as in the normal grid method, but in this case, the target grid forces the relevant distortion as dictated by the curved surface.

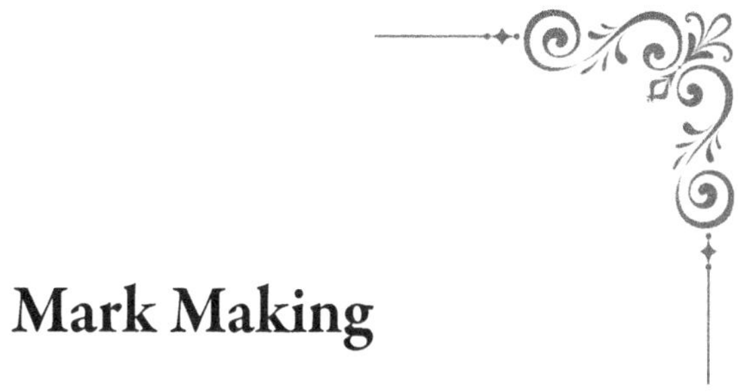

Mark Making

What follows is a description of several techniques of making marks on paper. Each has a particular quality and some are better for skin, while others are better for things like cloth or knitted-wool or wood.

Short lines

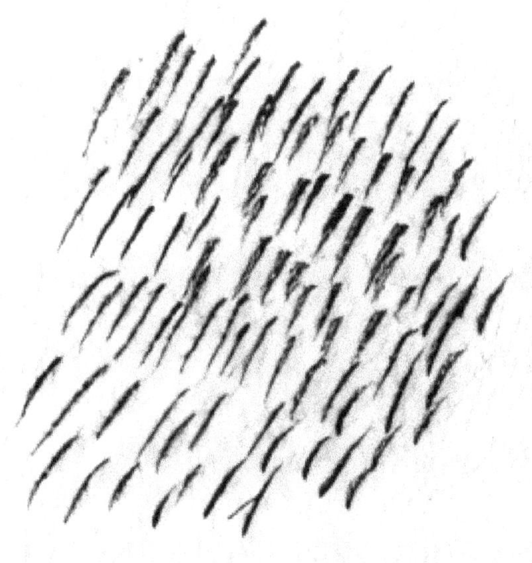

You might use short lines like this as part of a technique to build up texture—perhaps for a feather, some fabric, fur, whiskers and so on.

It's not exciting on its own but combined with other layers this will influence the overall texture.

Crosshatch

Cross-hatching is successful and you can use it alone to make a nice drawing. Tight crosshatching simulates dark values, and loose crosshatching simulates midvalues. If you draw the hatches to follow the underlying form this enhances the 3D effect. Crosshatching is unlikely to trick someone into thinking they are looking at a photograph unless the work is large, and it is viewed from a reasonable distance away. In that case, the eye will do optical mixing and the viewer will not be aware of the individual lines from a distance.

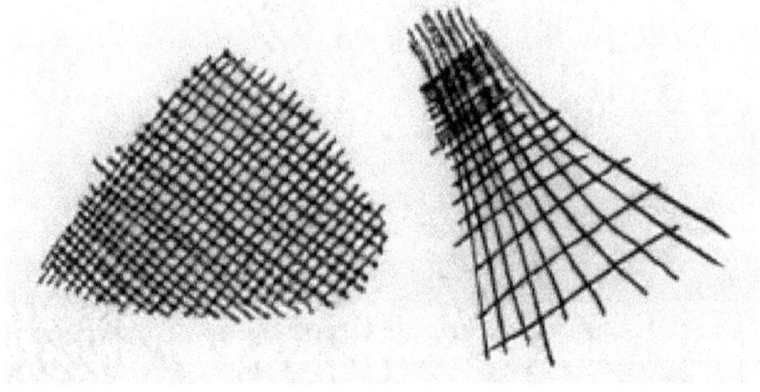

Smudging

Lay down a shape with a reasonably soft pencil, then take a blending tool and swipe it from the main mark off to one side. Repeat as required. This comet-like shape could form the base of a raised object and a shadow.

Circularism

Circularism is a good technique for skin. Some artists use only this method, but I like to add some random lines, some squiggles, some crosshatch and pointillism and smudging. Whatever seems right for the particular texture is good to try.

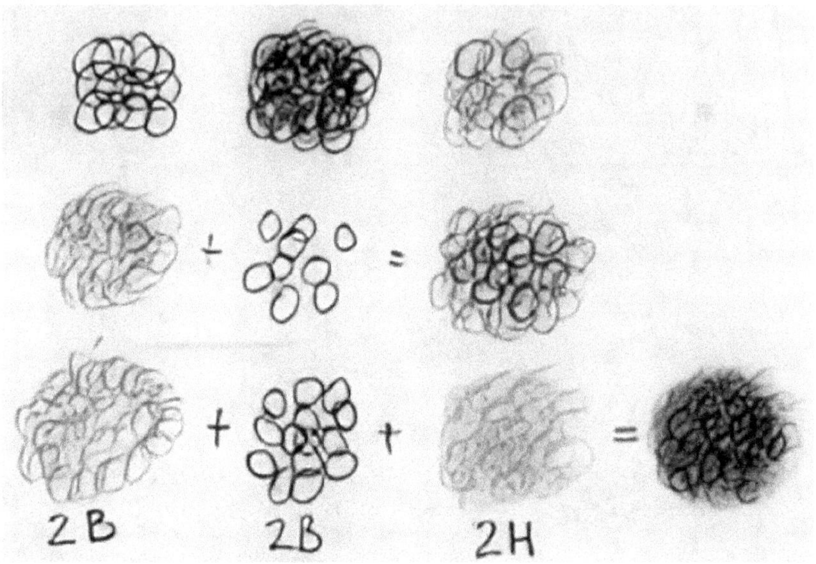

In this crude example the top row shows the basic technique which is simply to draw and overlap circles. Here, these are drawn darker than normal to let you can see the technique. The one in the middle of the top row uses the same technique but with more circles, and the one at the top right has lighter second layer.

The middle row shows you what you get by layering a light application and a few darker circles. The result has more texture.

The bottom row shows the combination of three layers and two pencil grades. Shown below is this technique in context. The stage shown is perhaps half finished. More layers and attention to filling the tooth of the paper will enhance realism. You can see how the circular technique starts to simulate skin. Little bumps and dips naturally start to appear. When this happens, use them by adding a slight shadow. Skin is not perfectly smooth, and these little imperfections make your rendering look more real.

The drawing below shows how skin texture develops using circularism. This particular drawing was a practice sketch so it was not developed completely but it's useful to see this half-finished stage.

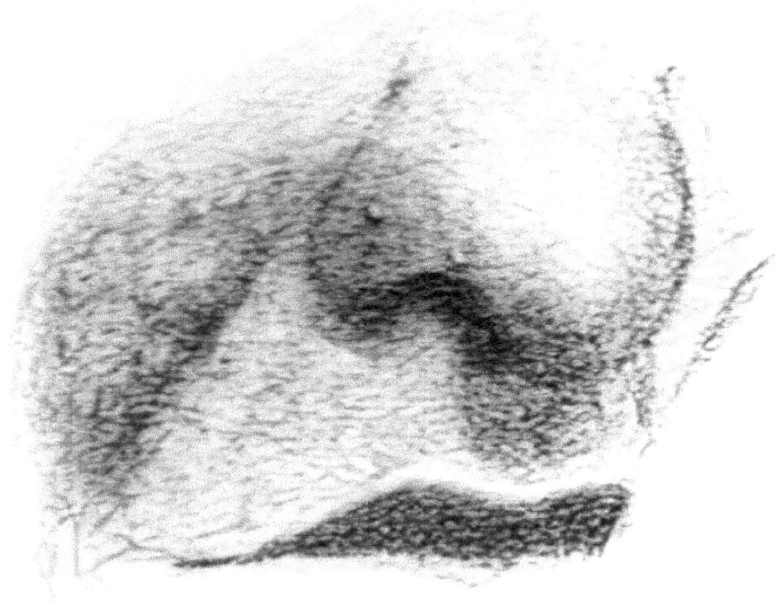

Pointillism

Using little dots, you can simulate dark values by applying them close together, and light values by spacing them out more. Each individual dot can have the same value, although they don't have to be similar. They don't even have to be the same shape or size.

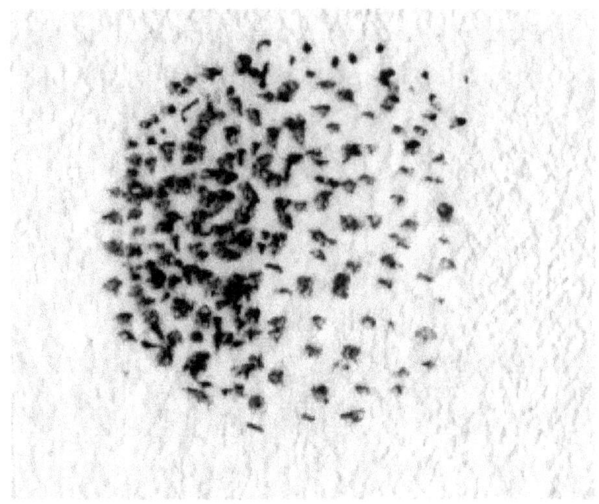

Application of graphite dust

You can easily make graphite dust using sandpaper as shown below.

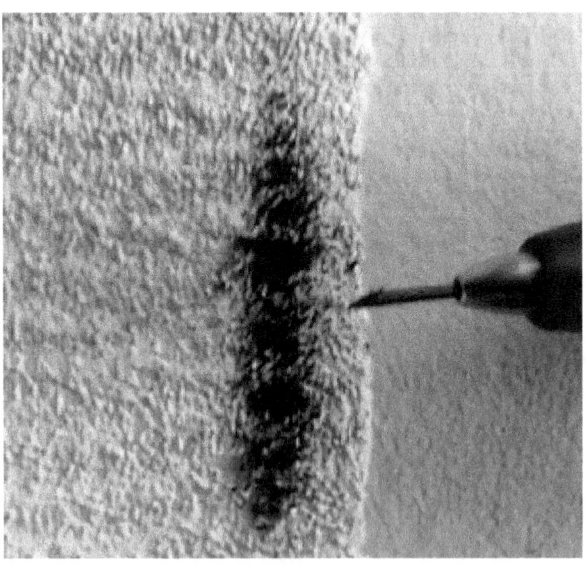

Then tip it onto your drawing and use a blending tool to work it into the paper.

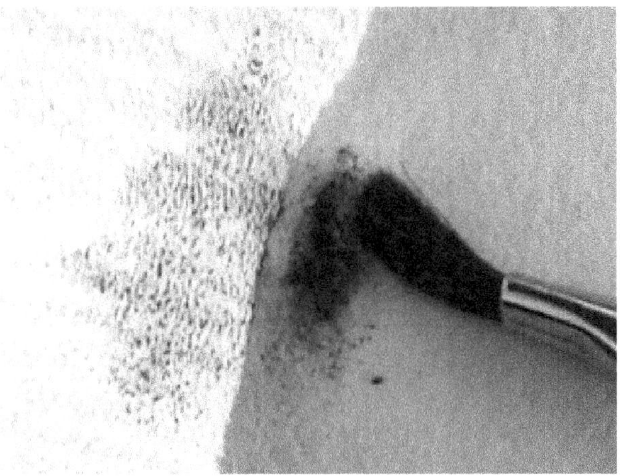

Veiling

I call this technique veiling because I employed it to draw a wedding veil.

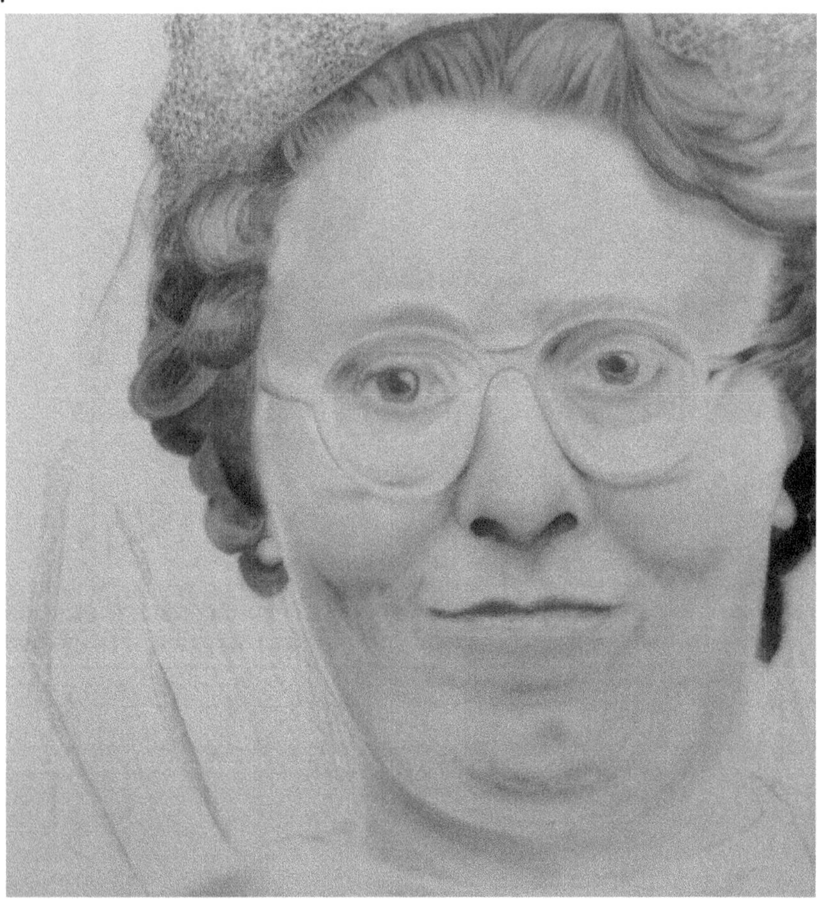

The veil is light and translucent. It would be difficult and time consuming to try to draw something like this with a point. I took the lead out of the mechanical pencil, laid it flat on the paper and dragged it around and up and down. No further work was needed for this effect.

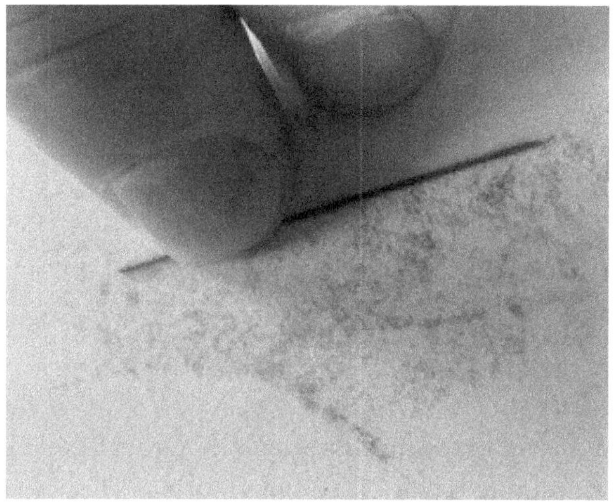

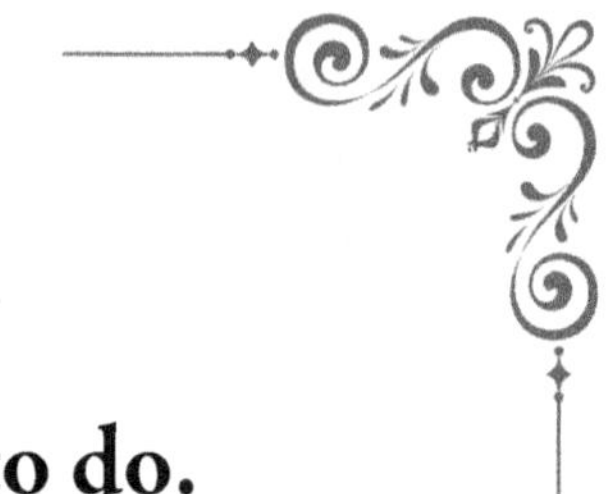

Things for you to do.

Observe.

For all artists, observation is a key skill. Even that famous and controversial pile of bricks shown in the Tate gallery in London in 1976 by Carl Andre required keen observation. That piece of work happened to involve more observation about society and the art world in general than a specific object, but nonetheless the act of observation was certainly a key factor.

Let's get back on topic and more specific. For you to become better at rendering realistic portraits, you will need to observe many features of the human face. The most important of these is light and shadow. These two elements of drawing (or painting) are what define form and texture. Some simple but important observations follow:

Mouth

Light normally comes from above. When light comes from above, the top lip looks darker than the bottom lip. The bottom lip is usually more rounded and therefore catches the light to produce highlights. The skin on the lips is crinkled because this skin needs to stretch easily, and you will need to differentiate this texture from the skin around. There is usually a vague highlight along the top of the upper lip. Teeth are typically in shadow and curve away towards the edge. As they do this, they become darker. Teeth are much darker than a naive representation will show because without proper observation, we draw what we know (teeth are white) compared with what we see (teeth are in shadow).

In the photograph below, I've exaggerated these observations on the right-hand side.

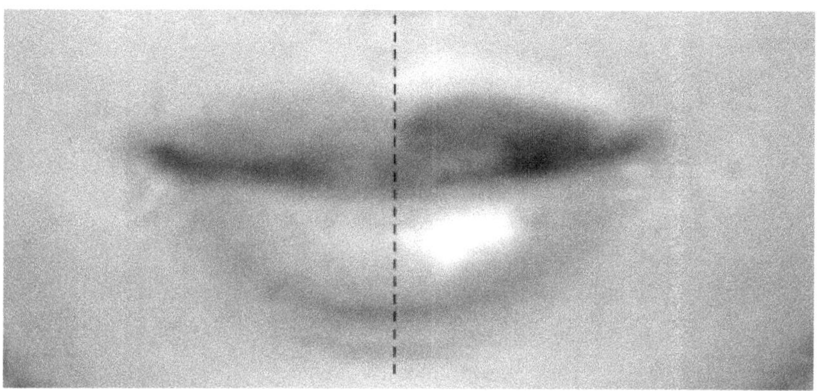

There is also a shadow under the bottom lip. If you don't reproduce this shadow, the lower lip will look like it is flat and glued to the face like a piece of paper. There is a smudge-like shadow in the corner of the mouth.

Techniques to represent this in a drawing include: Short lines for lip texture, followed by blending. You need:

- hard and soft pencils to get the required range of values;
- a smudge technique for the shadows in the corners of the mouth;
- some blending on the top lip to push graphite into the tooth;
- a kneadable eraser to lift out the highlights on the lower lip and above the top lip.

Blend the teeth-shadows. Use circularism on the skin. Reproduce the gentle transitions between the two textures of the lips and surrounding skin because hard lines are never present.

We need to repeat careful observation for other key features.

Nose

I've exaggerated some key observations about the nose on the right-hand side of the following photograph.

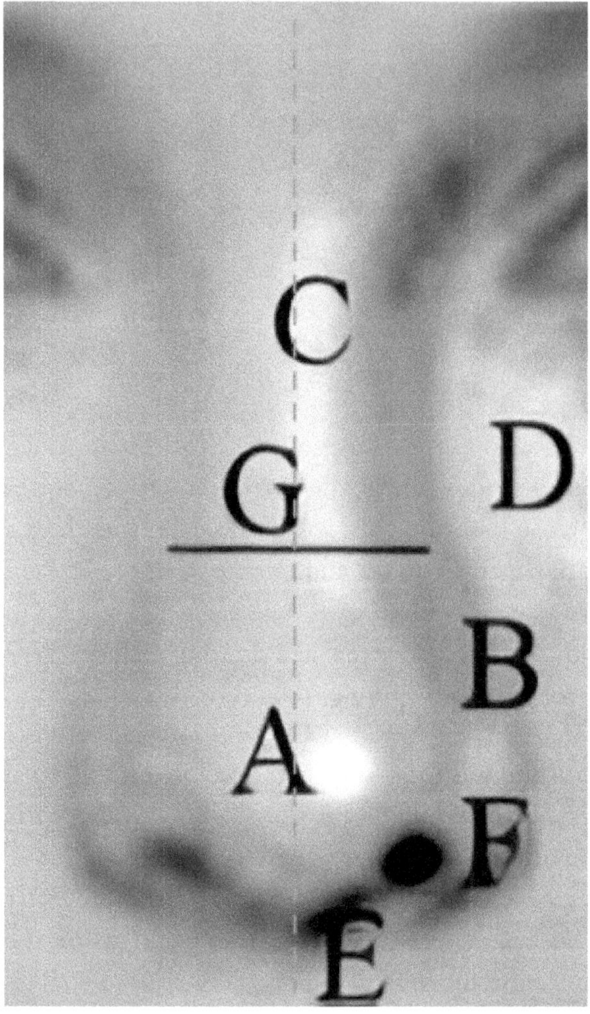

Small holes like nostrils appear dark. This darkness is most pronounced the deeper you see into the hole so the shadowing graduates from top to bottom when the light is coming from above.

The nose sticks out and catches the light in four main places. Since skin is reflective. In strong directional light, the tip of the nose can display a strong highlight (A). The lobes have a more muted highlight (B). There is a subtle highlight vertically along the nose from the bridge to the tip (C), and another muted one at the beginning of the cheek (D).

The sides of the nose graduate smoothly from highlight to highlight (G). If you represent this transition too strongly, the nose will look like it is a block. Noses can be difficult. They are never perfectly symmetrical, and yet too much asymmetry hugely alters the look of the face and affects likeness.

Eyes

Eyes are important and interesting because they move within the body. They are said to be direct paths into an animal's brain. There is much to observe about the eye and I will discuss some of them now. An eye is quite a large ball, and therefore there is a significant form to represent both what is exposed, and what is under the skin.

I've annotated this photograph with the numbers 1 to 7 to make it easier to discuss.

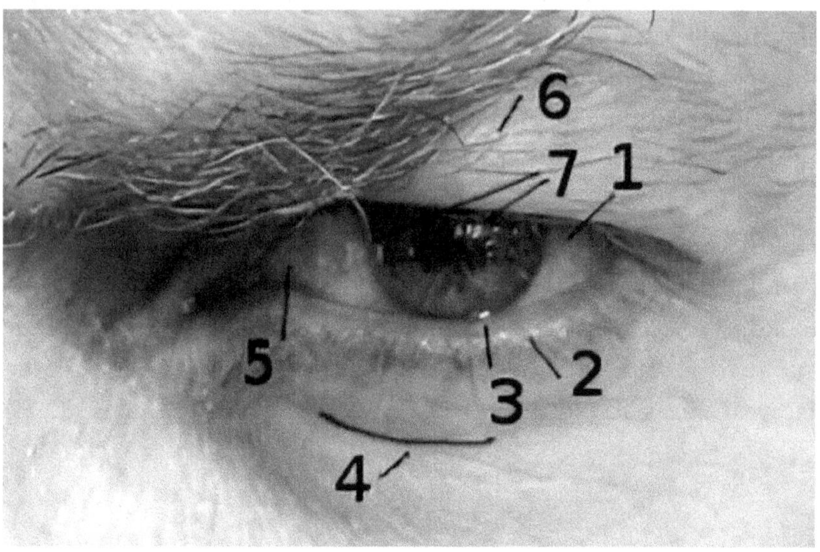

The top eyelid casts a shadow over the eye.

1. The lower lid has an irregular highlight.
2. The eye is moist and will catch a bright highlight at a point depending on the source of light.
3. The eyeball extends under the skin to this area and this causes the round form which makes the shadow above the line that I drew above the number 4.
4. The eyeball form falls away from the source of light into the corners of the eye and is therefore in shadow.
5. The upper brow has a muted highlight because the muscle under the eye forces the lid to protrude.
6. There are usually several sharp reflections in the eye that literally mirror the surroundings. Many beginners who notice a highlight at all and try to reproduce it simply put a single white dot. Although this can be effective and brings the eye to life, it is rather boring and is typical only of a staged studio shot. Look for more complex reflections, and remember the

eye is a curved surface.

Also note the creases around the eye. Draw these not with lines but with transitions. You can also see how the skin seems to have a grain—like wood has a grain. It's most clear below the number 4 on this photograph. In fact, the whole human body has different grain directions all over. Where visible, take note of this because it affects where creases form, and how the skin stretches.

Inside the eye, the pupil is not perfectly round; neither is the iris. The iris has an interesting texture that is made from tiny little elongated oval structures. The pupil is usually the darkest value. Some slight veins are visible in the whites of the eye. The whites of the eye are never white. In fact, the whites of the eye are only slightly lighter on average than the surrounding skin. Many beginners leave these areas perfectly white and it looks odd.

Note also how the eyebrow casts a shadow and is made from short unruly stiff little hairs.

In bright light, the pupil is small (as in the photograph above). In dim light, the pupil widens. In general, wide pupils are considered more attractive—especially in babies and ladies.

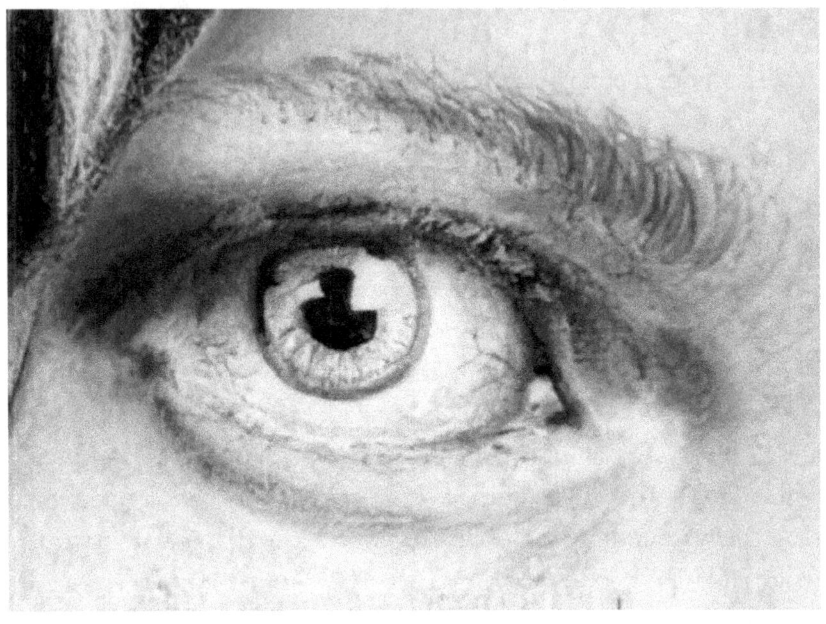

Even for a lady's eye, the eyelashes are usually not prominent. Over-displaying eyelashes can look false.

Ears

Ears used to baffle me. I have a drawing of ears that I apparently did at four years old so it seems to be a life-long struggle. Ears are awkward because the shapes don't fit into any particular classification.

The best way to draw an ear is to break it down into components. Most of these components are shadows, not highlights. The drawing below shows an ear broken into components A to F can be reassembled and rendered realistically.

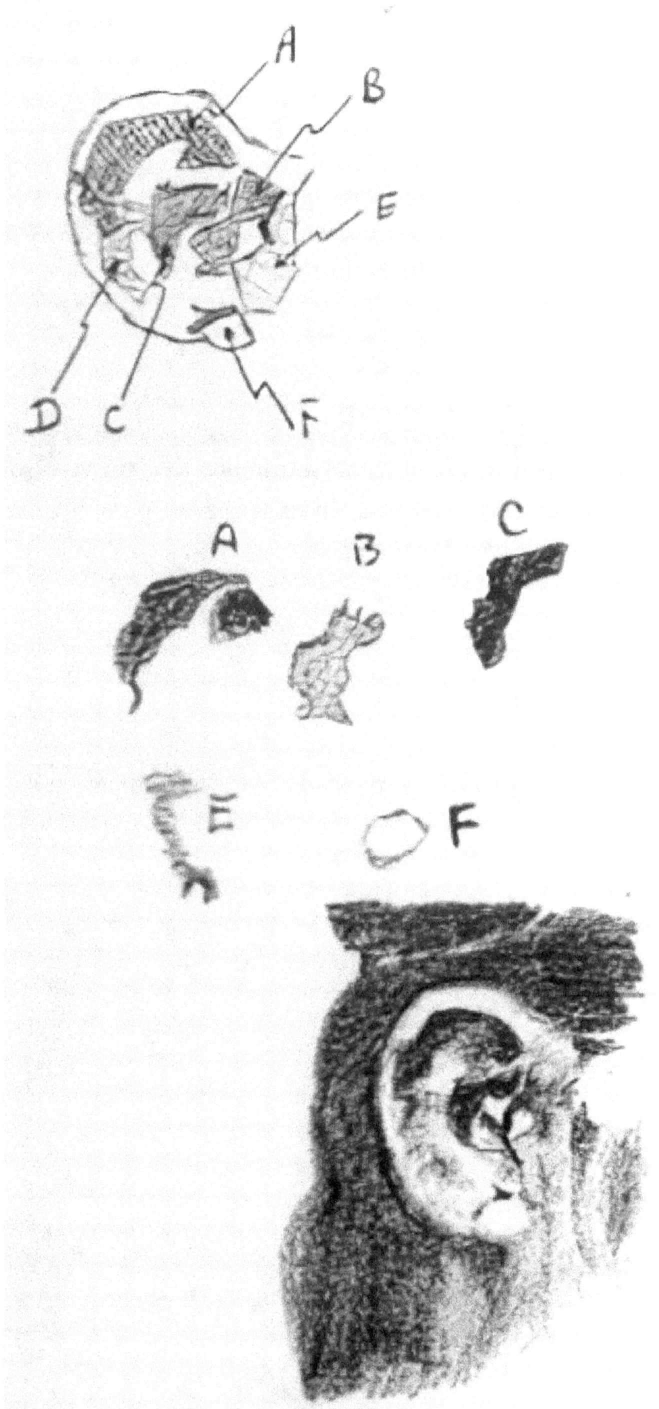

I don't have names for these shapes because they are different for each person's ear.

In the drawing above, we pull out shadows as abstract shapes and draw them independently as an exercise. Then we put them back together and note the spaces between these shapes are actually highlights. After that, join these shapes to the highlights with transitions and magically, a convincing ear will appear.

Hair

When drawing hair, many beginners draw what they know and not what they see. People know that a hair is a thin line that sprouts from the scalp and falls over the head to a tip dangling in space. To draw using that idea leads to an unconvincing result.

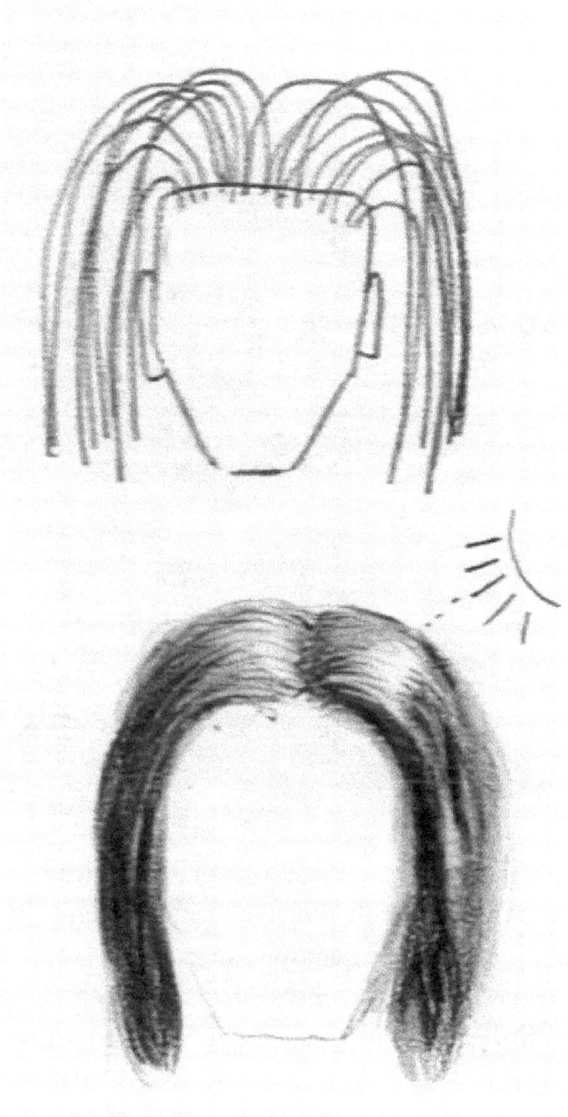

The upper illustration shows what we know about hair, and the lower one is closer to what we actually see. Hair is made up of curved surfaces and you rarely see a single hair. Sometimes you might see part of a single hair if it catches the light and depicting these by picking them out with an eraser can be effective. Below is a more carefully rendered example.

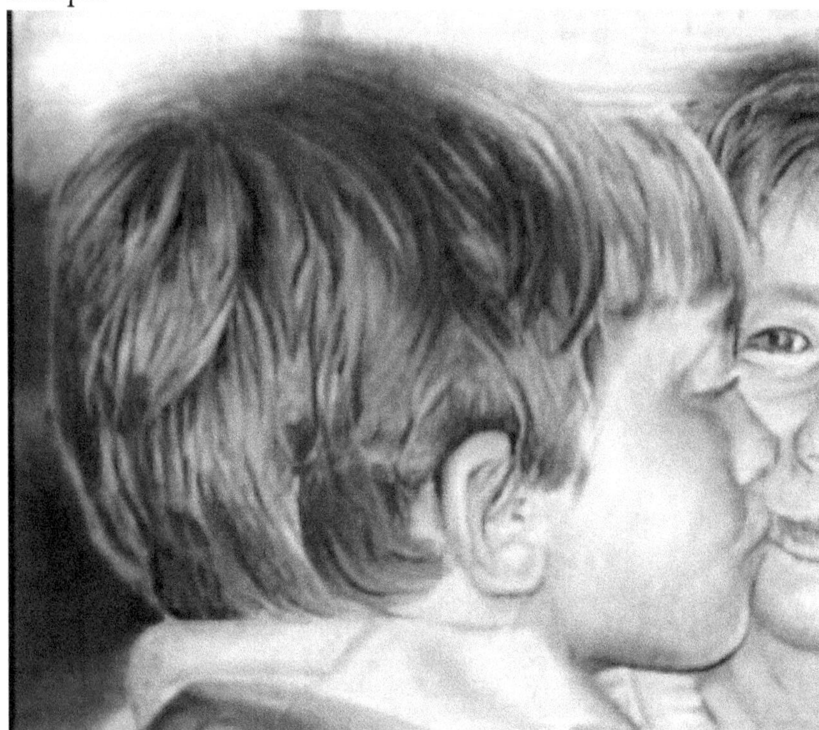

The light comes from the top right. There are shadows throughout, and in general, it is shapes not lines that make up the illusion. I used a combination of hard and soft pencils and a little blending. The shapes are present in hair because they stick together in groups. Since they are so fine, you cannot see the individual hairs—only the gross shapes are visible. These shapes are layered which is why you see one layer shadowing another. The shapes are curved surfaces and reflect light in the way you expect from a curved surface. Circularism is not a good technique for straight hair. Use short lines as the basic texture stroke but don't depict individual lines.

Find and note some visual clichés.

To produce good art is significantly dependent on being original but finding original ideas is hard. An exercise that you can do that will help your creativity is, ironically, to find as many examples of visual clichés as you can. This arms you with a good intuition about what is old and tired. Once you can easily recognise what is old and tired, it allows you to dream up new ideas.

A good trick for creativity is to get into a relaxed state. It's not easy to be creative when stress levels are high and there are a lot of distractions. Learn to meditate. Keep a notepad near you—even near the bed. If you get any ideas, jot them down. Especially jot down ideas that come from a near dream-like state. Try combining these and other ideas together. For example, you could look up two words at random. There are a few sites on the internet that generate words at random. Here are some random word-pairs:

Contradiction: Overlap

Evaluation: Holder

Type: context

Winding: Vacation

Tin: Island

This amazing exercise really helps you to break away from normal. The last word pair is particularly inspiring. As soon as I saw it, I visualised a seascape of an island where all the rocks and mountains were constructed of baked-bean cans without the labels present. It would be interesting to see how this scene could use the shape of a can, to make its reflections and ridges into an organic landscape. There could be a message to convey from this, like something against littering or something about the infiltration of man into remote islands. The possibilities are endless. This is where the so-called right-brain activity comes into play; but you need those left-brain techniques to have the skills to tie it all together. You would need to know how to play the light onto these man-made structures and fool the casual observer into seeing something natural.

Look how much detail you see in a shadow.

As mentioned earlier, photographs have a limited dynamic range. This means the difference in value between the darkest and lightest components is limited. When you look at objects outside in the bright sunlight, things that are bright are much brighter than you can capture in a photograph, and the number of values that you can see in a shadowed area is greater in real life compared with a photograph. In a photograph, the shadows are often all one value. The photographer could choose to expose the picture to reveal these shadow details, but that would be at the expense of hugely overexposing the highlights. The rest of the picture would look washed out. That's the limitation of a small dynamic range.

When you draw a picture, the upper value is limited by the colour and brightness of the paper while the darkest is limited by the tool. Carbon pencils or your homemade lampblack will give a good dark without getting shiny. It's not possible to get a graphite pencil dark and non-shiny.

But no matter which drawing medium you use, the darkest dark will appear in the deepest shadows. Within those shadows—despite what you might see in a photographic reference—there will be further subtle detail. The low end band of the value scale should be used within the shadow area.

Here is a simple 10-value scale where 0 is as black as you can get while 9 is the brightest white, and all the gradations between are evenly

spaced.

#0 is for the deepest darks.

#1 and #2 are for shadow details

#3, #4, #5, #6 are for midvalues.

#7 and #8 are for highlight areas.

#9 is for super-highlights. (The paper itself)

The photograph below has been converted into a picture with only 10 distinct values.

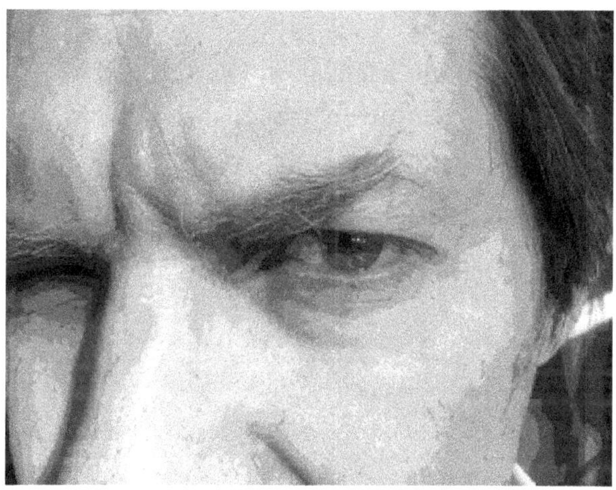

Look at the shadow areas in the hair. You can see some detail although it's not pronounced.

Create your own value scale.

The value scale helps you define the blackest black to paper-white as you need, using as many grades as you need. For a given paper, try different pencil grades and pencil strokes with the aim of creating a graduating scale without damaging the paper. With graphite, use many layers and never press too hard. This will avoid shine. Carbon and charcoal are not shiny.

The first six blocks from the left labelled 1 was created with an 8B grade pencil and blending. The three blocks labelled 2 were done without blending.

In the image above, a 6B pencil was used on Strathmore paper. The left block is a single layer without blending. Note how it does not fill the grain well. The values to the right were obtained using a layered blending technique.

The next example is a similar experiment using only an HB grade pencil.

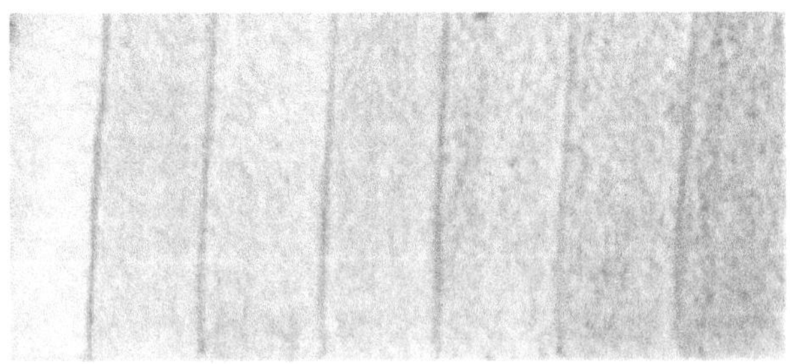

In this example, with more applications and careful filling of the paper's tooth, the HB pencil could produce a darker value but it will not be able to get as dark as the 6B pencil no matter what you try.

Introducing some texture

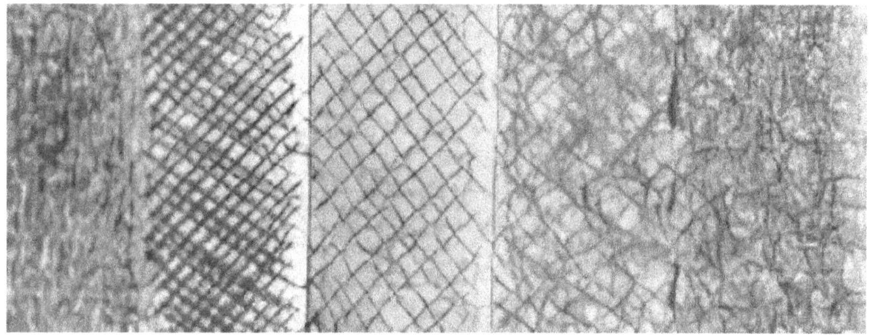

In this experiment, I used an HB pencil on Strathmore paper. The first block on the left is a single layer with no blending. Block two is simple crosshatching with no blending. The third is crosshatching with blending. The fourth is crosshatch, blending and circularism and the last block is the same as the one before but applied twice.

This is your first proper introduction to the layering technique. Note how even after only two applications of three techniques, the result starts to look like a textured surface rather than a sketch. You need to experiment with these layering techniques, and use different pencil points with different grades and marks to work out how to generate various textures.

Practice a gradual shade.

The value scale is practice for creating bands of various values. A gradual shade is practice for a fully practical technique. It is a fundamental skill for rendering realistic portraits, clothing and objects. When light strikes a surface, it almost always illuminates it in a non-uniform way and if we are to reproduce that, we need to shade gradually from dark to light. Even a wrinkle in skin or an edge of some object has gradual shading from light to dark. A rapid gradation is seen on an edge, and a slow smooth gradation on a curved surface. Even a flat surface is unlikely to be evenly illuminated.

One of the best exercises is to draw an egg. We will do this in stages because there are three elements involved.

1. Main lighting
2. Shadows
3. Reflected lights

Let's explore the elements of an egg.

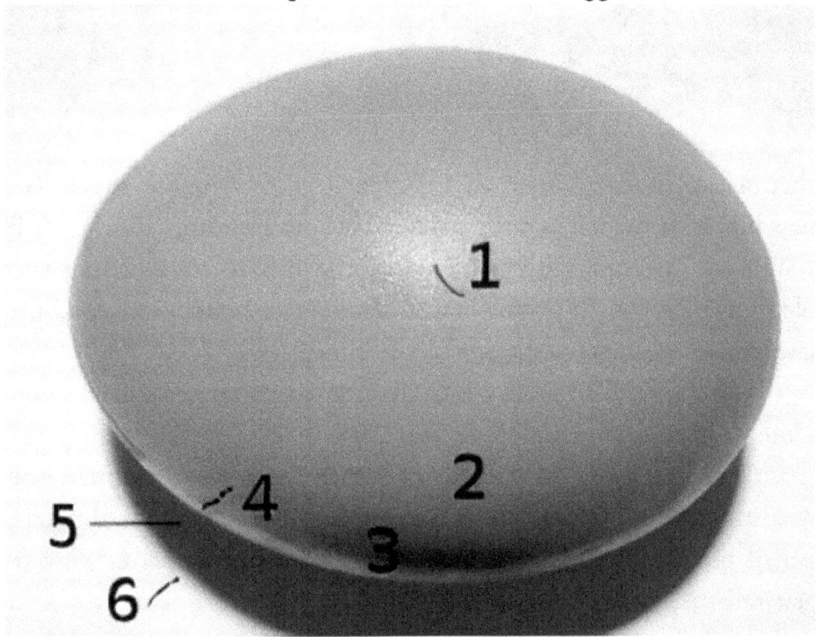

To observe the egg properly, we need to make mental notes. The texture is not perfectly smooth. This is most obviously seen in the highlight at #1. The way to draw this is to leave white paper for the highlight, then use a combination of blended hard graphite and dabs with the tip of a kneadable eraser. #2 is the area of midvalue and #3 is the shadow. You need to copy the transition from highlight through midvalue and into the shadow at #3. But also look at the reflected highlight #4. This light bounced onto the egg from the table-top. #5 is the main shadow and #6 is a fuzzy edge of the shadow which is caused by fringing.

Try to draw this egg as accurately as possible. By far the most difficult part is to get that gradual transition over the curved surface. You should also notice how the surface curves from left to right and top to bottom; therefore, as the light glances off it at an angle, rather than directly into your eye like the main highlight, the edges of the egg are deeper values. One final observation is that the edges of the egg are a little fuzzy. This is mainly because the camera has a limited depth of field. You can choose to copy that limitation, enhance it or ignore it.

This scenario can be complicated further by considering multiple main light sources, but at this stage we will only consider a single light source.

For most portraits, it is unlikely the actual source of light is in the picture. When the light source is actually in the frame, the drawing will have complex shadows, because the light source is close and will spray light across your picture from a wide range of angles; you will see reflected highlights off walls and the floor or ceiling.

If the light source is from the sun outdoors, or from a window, then the rays of light are practically parallel which makes the shadows simple, but there will still be reflected light from nearby objects. When the light comes from an overhead globe on a low ceiling, then the rays of light spray out from that point.

When you draw objects, you will need to consider from where the light source comes. Imagine the common trick with a hand-held torch where children hold a torch upright, and close to their chins to depict a spooky scene for telling horror stories. This scene contains complex and unusual shadows. It is a good exercise to try to draw something like this.

Unless you are using toned paper, and lighter pencils, you don't actually draw the light. What you are really drawing is shadow. The shadows depend mostly on the light source, but as mentioned, also on reflected light from objects nearby. It is reflected light which makes an object appear part of a group of coherent objects, and it is the shadows cast from your object onto surrounding surfaces which cements it into the scene.

Remember: Shadows are not hard blocks of darkness. The shadow is also a shaded element of your drawing, because reflected light and fringing will influence its appearance.

Contour Drawing Exercise.

A contour drawing is a line drawing. We don't draw lines when *rendering* portraits and I continually talk about transitions instead. A contour drawing is therefore a map of where transitions happen—like a visual note. When you think about this a little, it's not obvious where a transition should be represented by a line. For example where should the known edge of the object be? Is it where the value changes? If so, which of the ten values do you choose? Why are there ten values? Why not seven or forty? In the ten-value photograph above, the contours could actually be drawn each time the value changes, but in most circumstances we don't see distinct values because there is a continuous change from dark to light.

When doing a contour drawing try to locate and document value changes. It's important because it helps you get a unified tonal-range over the entire picture.

Here is a computer-assisted contour drawing using the above ten-value picture. Although there are algorithms to do edge-detection, they are not good for artistic uses. The output is too detailed and messy so I chose which lines to draw and where to draw them.

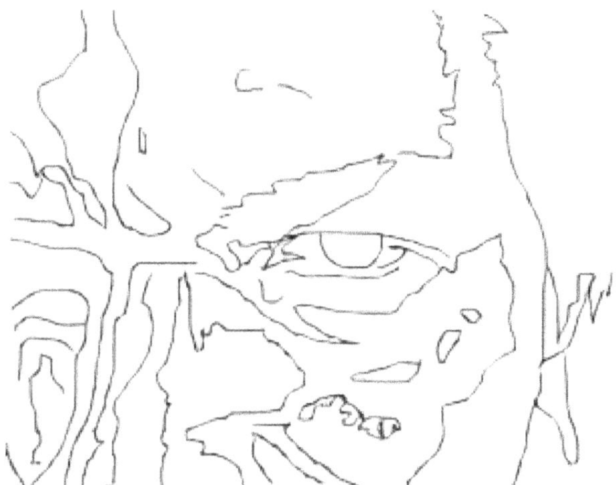

This might look familiar as it's like the paint-by-numbers method! You will need to render transitions across these lines.

Here is freehand example of a preparatory contour drawing. In this case, it is of two hands. Performing this exercise prepares the mind for a full rendering. You don't need to be accurate and it helps to do this by eye without measurements.

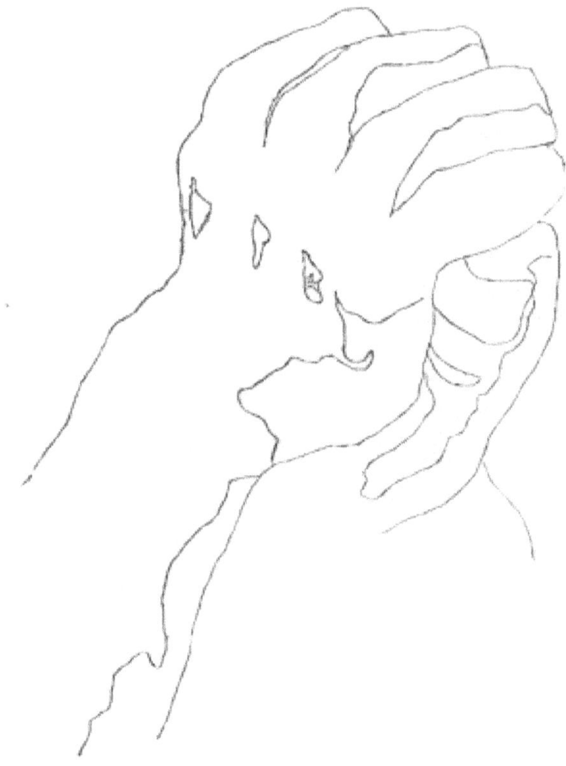

The final rendering of these hands and who owns them is shown below.

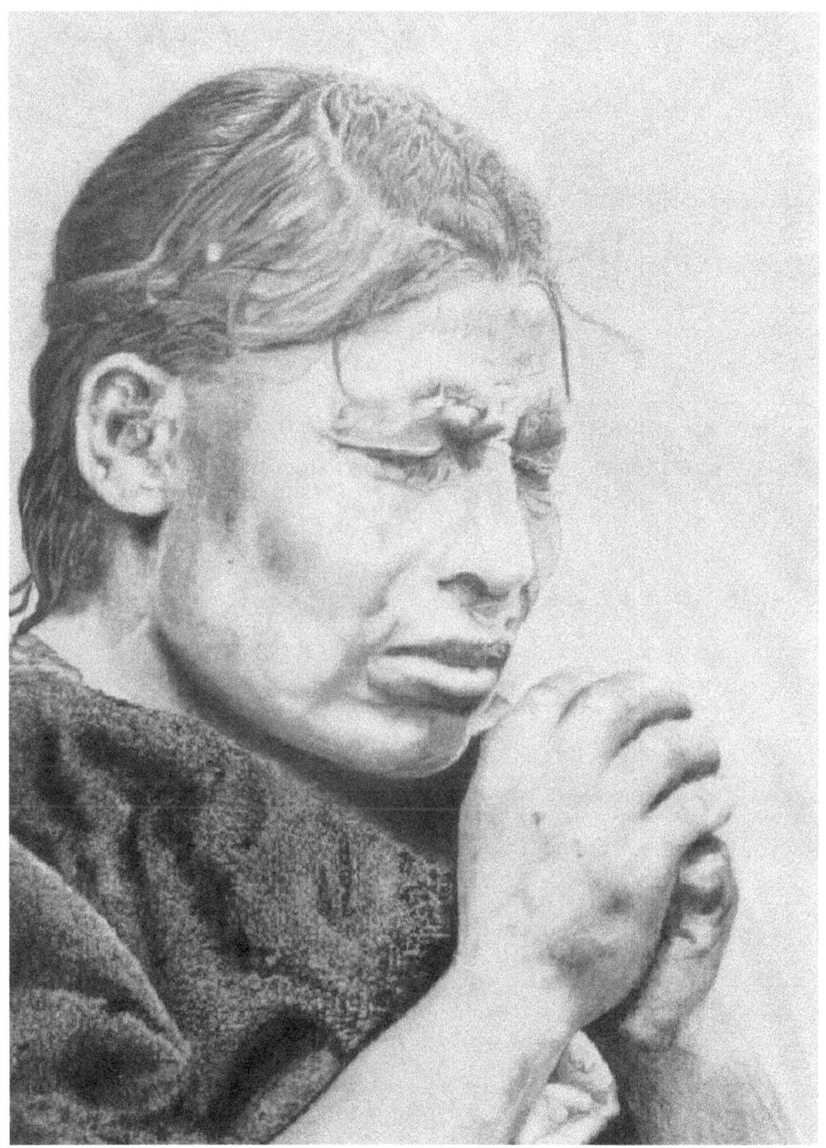

The transition line and more.

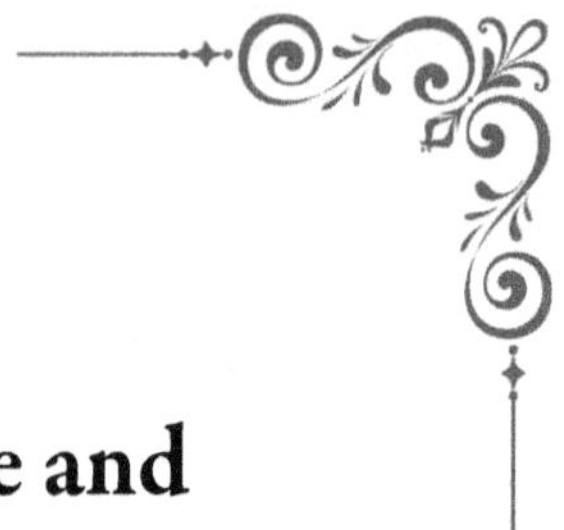

Draw a line without using lines. We will draw a line using circles. It's best to see this in pictures rather than try to describe it using words.

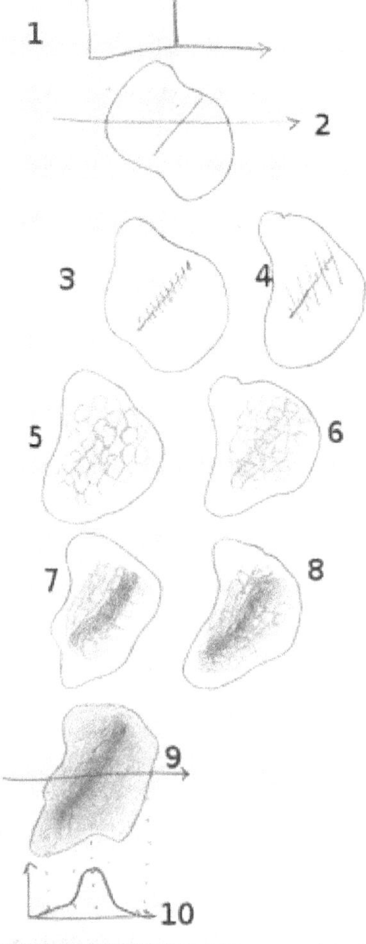

#1 is a graph of the intensity (value) of the line as it crosses the reference arrow. It is a single spike because this is a single line and has definite edges. #2 is a single line inside a boundary. #3 is a note-taking way to represent a line that is a little smeared out. #4 is another way to note a smeared-out line. You might use something like #3 and #4 in a rough sketch just to remind yourself of the extent of the transition. #5, #6, #7, #8 show the various layers progressing towards a reasonably convincing rendering of an area of skin with a crease as depicted in #9. The last rendering used a hard pencil over the top of the soft layers.

In graph **#10** we can see how the intensity (value) rises to a peak towards the crease, and then gradually falls away slowly after that. This is a good method for realistic creases below an eye because a single line would look illustrative and cartoon-like. Use the same technique throughout.Bumps and Dimples

Bumps and dimples are combinations of light and shadow. The illustration below shows a dimple on the left, and a bump on the right. But for this to be effective, there must be enough clues in the overall drawing to show that light comes from the top right. For this to work, all the other shadows in the picture must agree. Otherwise, it will be unconvincing or confusing to look at.

Try looking at the bump and dimple upside down. They will appear to lose form and might even swap where the bump looks dimple-like and the dimple turns into a bump. This is a powerful illustration that you are creating an illusion that is dependent on the workings of the human brain. We are conditioned to view form where light comes from above and it becomes confusing if shadows are in the wrong place.

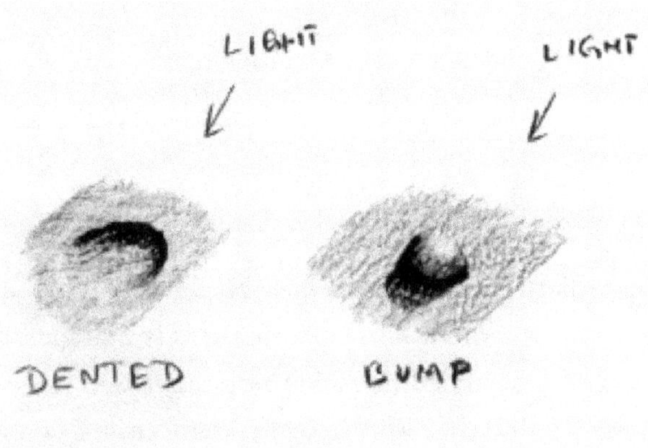

You can see the dimple has a shadow at the top right, nearest the light source, and a highlight furthest away. The bump has a highlight nearest the light and the shadow is cast furthest away. That's all there is to it.

When rendering skin, on a small-scale, these two structures are often seen as scars or moles or simply part of the architecture of a particular person's skin. These tiny details help to bring realism into a drawing. When you use the layered circularism technique, these little structures appear automatically. If it looks good, you can accentuate them with a dab from a kneadable eraser and a bit more shadow, or you can mute them away with the eraser if they don't make sense. To complete this little rendering tutorial, here are two surfaces. The first is flat, and other is curved. The flat one has no visible transition, while the curved one has graduated to black as the surface curves away from the light source.

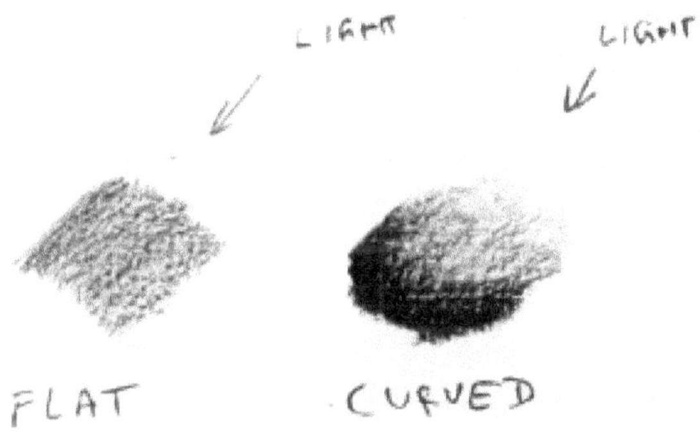

Where edges curve away from the source of the light, the surface darkens and so the edges darken. This means that front-lit objects often have dark edges, but a side-lit object will have one bright edge, and one dark edge. You should compare how the light strikes a surface rather than the actual placement of the surface relative to the other objects. The position of the light source is a major consideration. When you treat light properly, some dramatic effects can be brought to life in the finished work.

Locate abstract shapes

Cut out a 1cm square hole and explore abstract shapes within a realistic picture. Here is a reference picture.

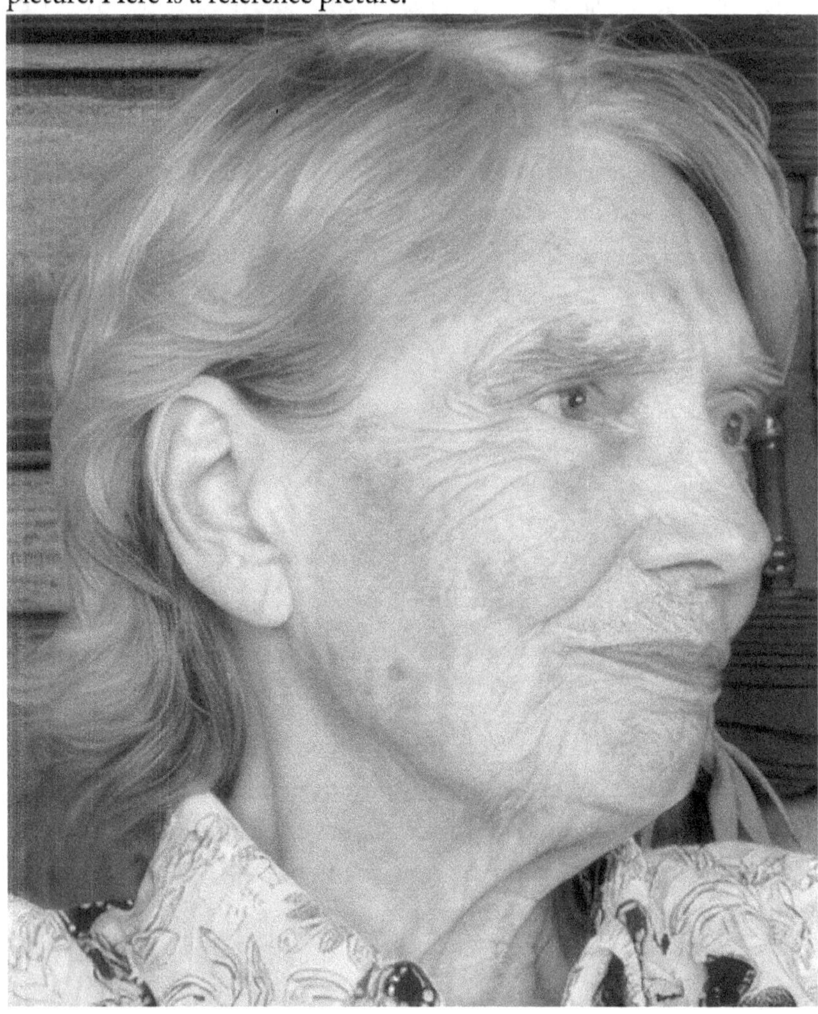

Next is the same picture with a small square viewing hole which we can move around to find abstract shapes.

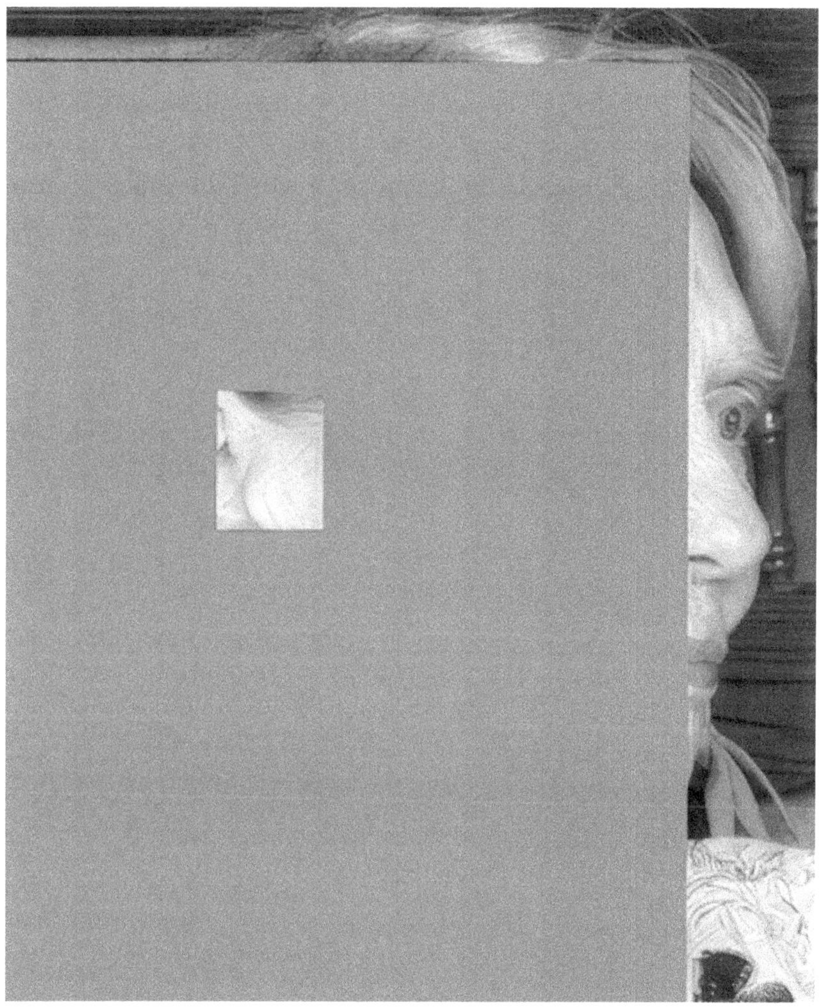

The effect is dramatic. It is a great way to train your eye and get you to observe the shapes, values and transitions of an object. Use the mask to isolate what you are drawing and copy what you see, not what you know. This works well for hair, creases, clothing and ears.

Reflections and shadows of shiny things.

Shiny and transparent things make some interesting shapes. The pair of glasses below dramatically illustrates the bizarre shapes cast from an oblique light source across a flat but patterned table. This particular photograph would make an ideal study for a student of graphite-rendering.

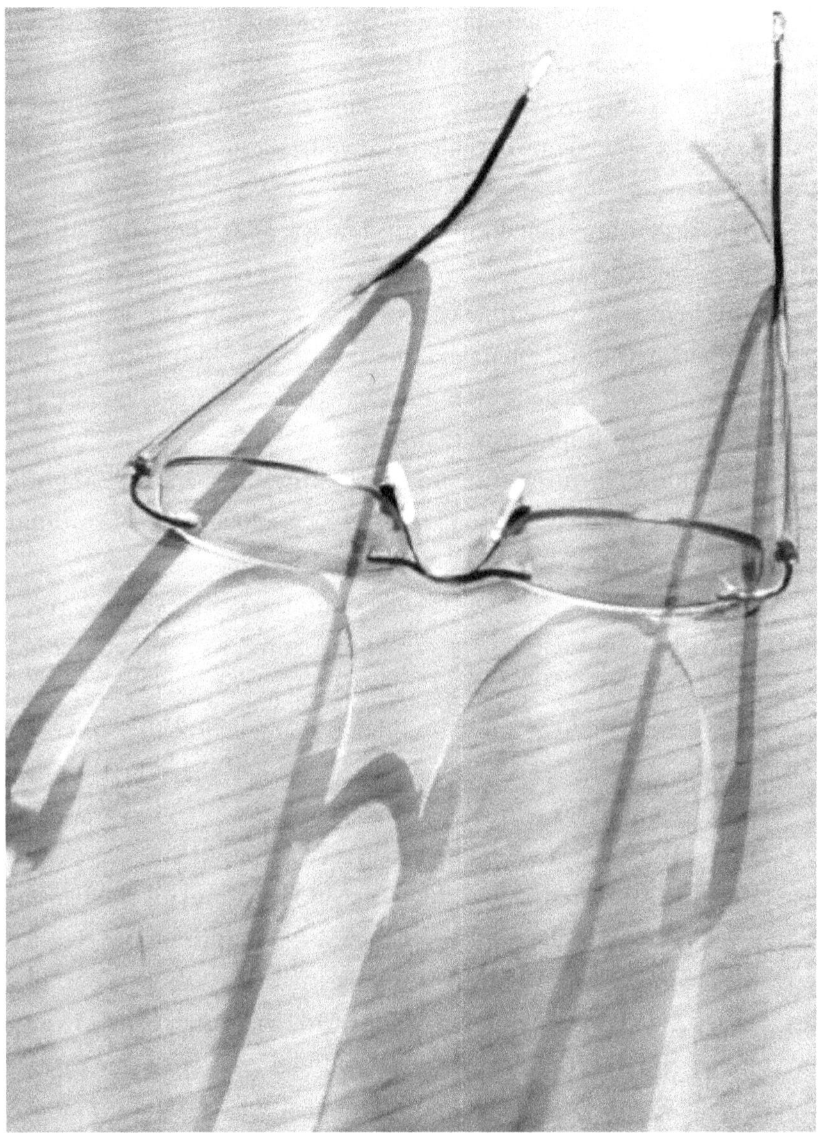

Let's begin our observations. The light is coming from the rear-right which casts shadows towards our view. The shadows of the arms are darkest, but you can still see the diagonal pattern of the table-top in these shadows. There are shadows cast from the rims of the glasses but they are not as strong.

There is a second light source in this picture, and it comes from behind the viewer. We can see this because there are clearly two shadows from the arms where they curl over ears. The secondary shadows are weak but noticeable once you take the time to observe them.

There is a curious reflection behind each lens. It's not immediately clear why that reflection is there but my guess is the lenses focus light from the light source behind the viewer. The main clue is that the one on the left is different to the one on the right and I suspect this is because of different lens strength and configuration. These are my glasses, and I have astigmatism in my right eye.

The shadows in front that are cast by the lenses are only slightly deeper values than the table-top and they have a reflective halo around them.

The lenses slightly distort the pattern on the table. Without these distortions, the lenses would either not appear to be present, or would look like flat glass.

There are a couple of super highlights bouncing off the rims. The darkest value is in the arms that hook over ears, and the lightest on the little pads that fit over the nose.

That probably completes the left-brain analysis of this scene. The extended and distorted shapes of the shadows stimulate right brain activity. When you look at this in a new way—that is in a more creative way, the shape of these shadows is provocative. They almost look like little independent ephemeral flat beings with their own little life and personality. The left one seems to be holding hands with one on the right. Each seems to be holding its free arm up in the air, perhaps holding a water hose to pore water gently from the ends.

Finally, there are interesting negative spaces. These are the spaces between the shadows and components of the glasses. The composition of this picture is not too far away from being a reasonably strong abstract artwork. In the transformation below, a computer program was used to apply a filter called 'Neon'. It's not important what that actually means, but it is interesting how the result could serve well as a starting point for a full colour abstract work or a high contrast monochromatic work. The 'essence' of the spectacles on the table is still somehow tenuously visible, but the angled lines and shapes dominate in an abstract manner and the pattern of the table-top has somehow transformed into a surface that suggests rippling water. The dark shadows on the right provide an impression of a textured surface. This basic pattern could easily be developed into something striking in an original work of art.

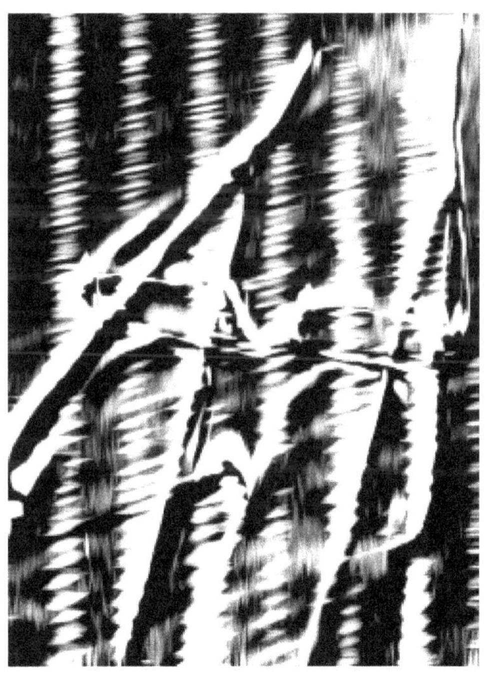

Here is another shiny object. In this case it is a white mannequin found in a shopping centre. It's a good example to show the difference between normal transitions that you find on human skin compared with a hard shiny surface. By this I mean they are more like lines compared with what you would ever find on a more textured surface and therefore the transitions are fast.

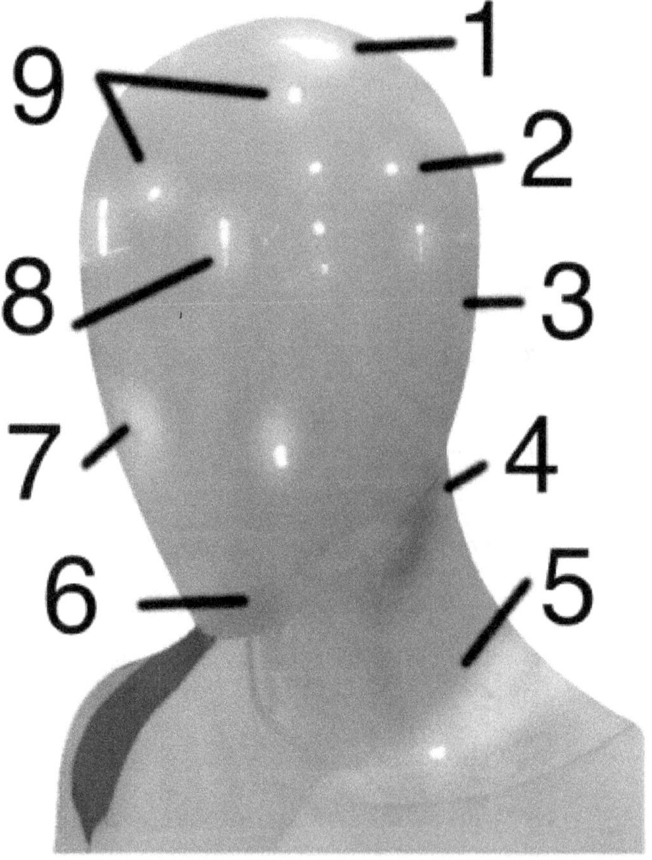

It's instructive to examine shiny surfaces. One obvious characteristic of a shiny surface is its smoothness. To depict a smooth surface, you need techniques that don't make noticeable pencil marks. You also need to fill the tooth of the paper completely, and evenly. A smooth continuous curve is challenging to render properly as you need to control the values from light to dark carefully. Try blending with a paint brush in this situation.

In the photograph of the mannequin, let's look at some of the features. The highlight at **#1** is well-defined. It has sharp edges and corners, and it follows the curve of the surface. This highlight is most likely coming from a skylight. **#2** and **#9** show small round spots and these are most likely coming from individual down-lights in the ceiling of the shopping centre. **#3** points to a value that is dark for an object that is actually a bright white. This dark value is there because less light bounces back into your eye from that angle. **#4** is a subtle form shadow. The change in value is almost imperceptible but it's definitely a feature and if you wanted to draw this object, that shadow would be important. **#5** points to a curved value-boundary. If we did a contour drawing of this mannequin, that would be one of the contours. Again, this is a subtle change in value but the shiny surface means it is sharp and abrupt. This boundary actually marks a light shadow area under the chin that extends around the neck. **#6** points out a change in value due to less light hitting that area perpendicularly. Compare this value with that of the shadow under the neck. It is almost identical. **#7** brings your attention to a light highlight. There are other similar values in this picture and they are from more distant, less intense sources of light. **#8** points to a bright vertical reflection from a doorway that leads outside the shopping centre.

To draw this object, you would need apply marks gently then blend some medium grade graphite, and keep working it until you get the subtle values in place that make it look 3D. This could take a lot of effort and it's not an easy exercise. Since there is no significant texture, you don't need to apply a texture-layer. If this object were made of cloth, you would start with marks that simulate the weave of cloth, and then lay down a layer to give it form. When you have the form correct, add those highlights, using an eraser mask to give a sharp quick transition. Then use a hard pencil to dim the highlights to the correct value.

Even though this object is bright white, all the reflections of the surroundings in the shiny surface make it average to a mid-grey value. It's only the highlights that suggest the bright white surface.

More texture practice

Texture is a description of the surface of an object. We have seen that circularism is effective for skin. This is because skin cells are small, irregular, roughly circular shapes; so our general action to draw overlapping circles naturally brings out suitable texture. Straight hair has different texture.Although we know that you can't see individual hairs from a distance, the fact they all combine in bundles makes a complicated surface with an underlying pattern of lines. If hair were in tight curls, the base is made from curved lines.

Brick has a sharp rough texture and the underlying mark for brick or similar could be dots, or irregular blotches. If the texture on brick is pronounced, and the light oblique and sharp, every irregular bump would cast a long irregular shadow. You would need to find a technique that simulates this. In this last case, the shadows might be most dominant which could mean that short bold deep dark angled strokes would work well as the underlying texture layer.

If you are simulating knitting, the texture will be formed from a combination of lines, little V shapes and shading.

To render a knitted sweater, once you get the technique of simulating texture, you still need to consider form. To do this, lay down the texture layer, then use another technique—perhaps a random squiggle—to darken areas in shadow and deepen the values where the clothing recedes into the background. Then you might lift some of the pattern in selected areas for the highlights. By doing it this way, some texture is left both in the shadows and the highlights.

Here are some more practice-doodles for mark-making, texture and form. You should do these experiments regularly. Note how the rendered forms stand out from the page while the basic textures lie flat. This illusion is because of the shadows and highlights.

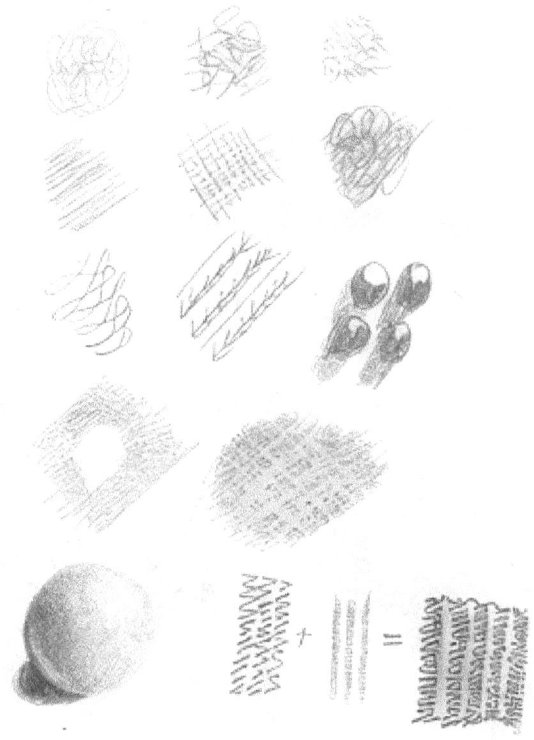

The next illustration shows the construction of texture and shading for a rough wool suit. This demonstrates a lot of what we have discussed so far. The shape of the pencil point is flat and sharp. You use the edge of that sharp point to create a series of tight zig-zags.

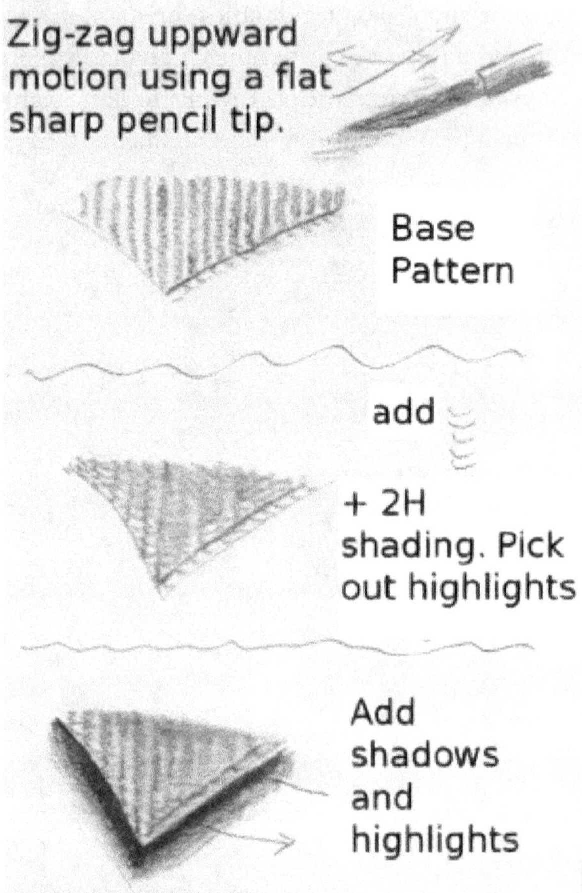

These zig-zags create layer-1 for the base pattern. A second layer adds some cup-shapes. This simulates stray fibres of the rough wool suit and randomises the pattern to make it look more natural. Finally, a 4H glaze helps to unify the texture, and then shadows are added with a 2B pencil. Highlights are picked out with the eraser.

Practice organic forms.

Drawing eggs can get boring quickly. But you can use the basic shape and skill-set to put together organic forms. These don't need to represent anything in particular, but they are fun to do and great practice. It's possible to produce a finished work of art just using these skills.

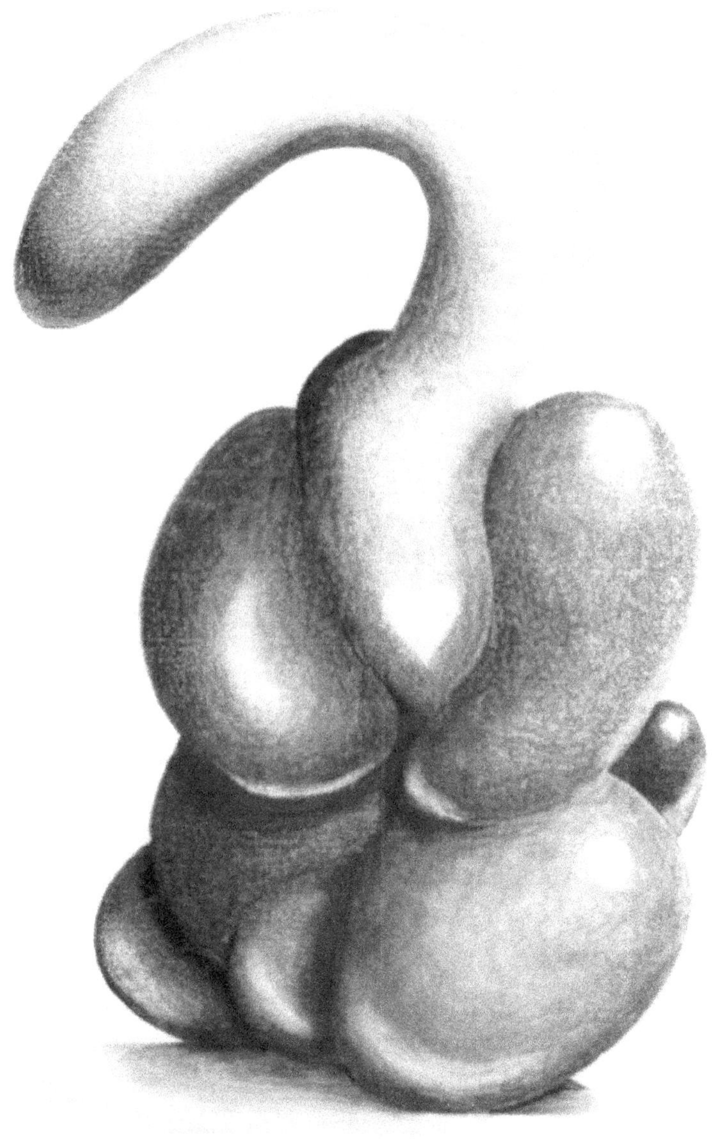

I call this piece "Abstract Ted". He has some dark textures, some quite bright highlights, smooth organic forms, reflected light, shadows and a pleasing composition. The underlying texture of the paper is rough and this shows through in the final piece.

Now let's take a close look at something as mundane and common as a paper napkin. This is where you can practice new powers of observation not only about texture, but also light, shadow, form, and recognition of abstract shapes.

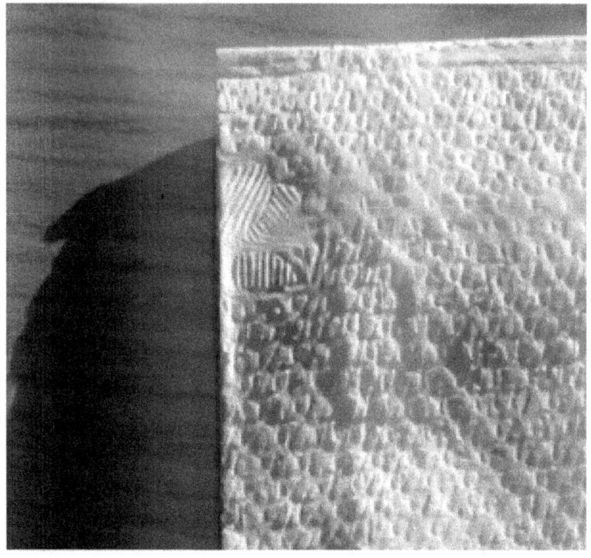

The main shadow is obvious. Its position will dictate how far off the page the napkin appears to be. The shape of the edge of the shadow is exaggerated compared with the edge of the napkin because of the oblique light source. The napkin is white, but most of it is depicted with midvalues. There are many small highlights. Additionally, there are three main textures. The main texture looks like a raised bump but there is an embossed set of lines in one area, and the edge of the napkin has a different texture. There is a dominant pattern that looks slightly like honeycomb. This pattern could start your drawing as construction lines. Don't draw them heavily as these lines are not really there. They emerge as an illusion from the overall pattern and are only implied in the overall picture.

Now we are ready to take a look at the abstract nature of these features. A closer look will help:

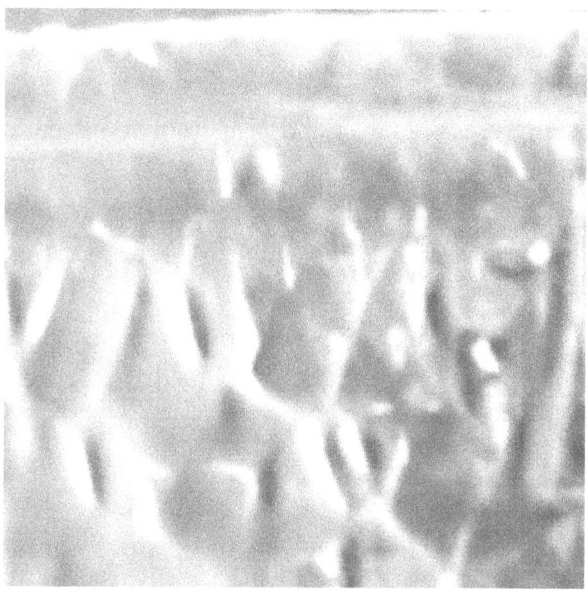

You should look at this in terms of positive and negative space, and as dips and bumps. We already know how to make dips and bumps because we practiced them earlier. The light comes from the top right, so when you see a shadow to the right of a highlight, it is a dip. When the shadow is to the left of a highlight, it's a bump. We can also start to think about layers.

The first layer could be a medium grade graphite dust, pushed into the tooth of the paper using a small soft brush. The second layer could be to use a kneadable eraser and wander about dragging it and dabbing it roughly as you see in this small sample. A third layer would be to put in those little shadows. Put some to the right of the highlights for dips, and some to the left for bumps. Don't overdo the contrast because as we noted earlier, the majority of this white napkin needs midvalues.

That's all there is to it. It's nowhere near as complicated as it might seem if you were to tackle it without the initial (left-brain) analysis. The right-brain activity comes when you start to wander about the work with the kneadable eraser. This is when you can zone out, listen to music, and go with the creative flow. There is no point at all in mechanically replicating the actual pattern that you see. You need to find a way to capture the essence and suggestion of that pattern. When viewed from a distance it will look pretty good.

Two final layers will finish this off properly. At a larger scale, the average value will vary because the napkin is not perfectly flat. To unify the drawing, use the glaze-technique over those parts that have an overall lower value. Be sure to use transitions to render creases. In the final layer, use an eraser to gently dab out broad average areas—leaving hints of detail. This will raise the value where the light source is near perpendicular to the surface. You might need a dirty kneadable eraser to gently lift these areas.

Render an ear

Here is a picture-tutorial to show all the stages I used to render an ear. The first stage is to lay down a light layer into which is drawn the next layer with an eraser.

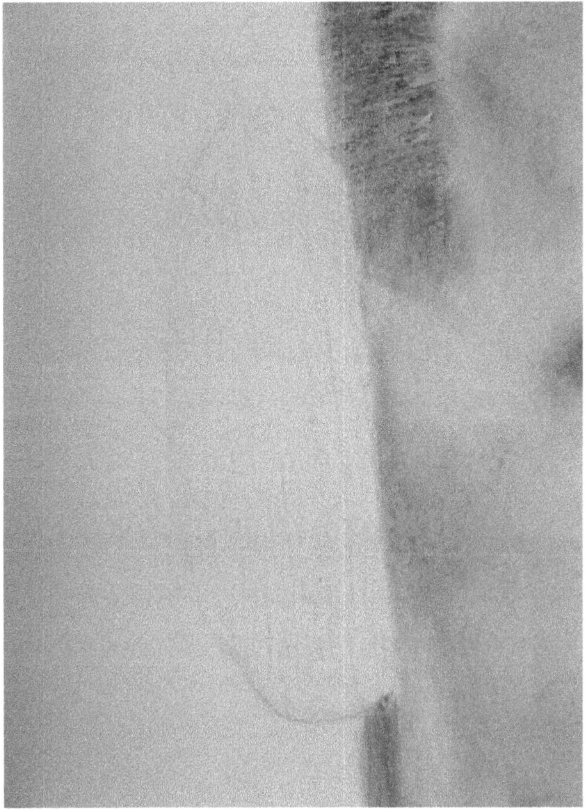

I used a kneadable eraser to pick out the parts of the ear that catch the light.

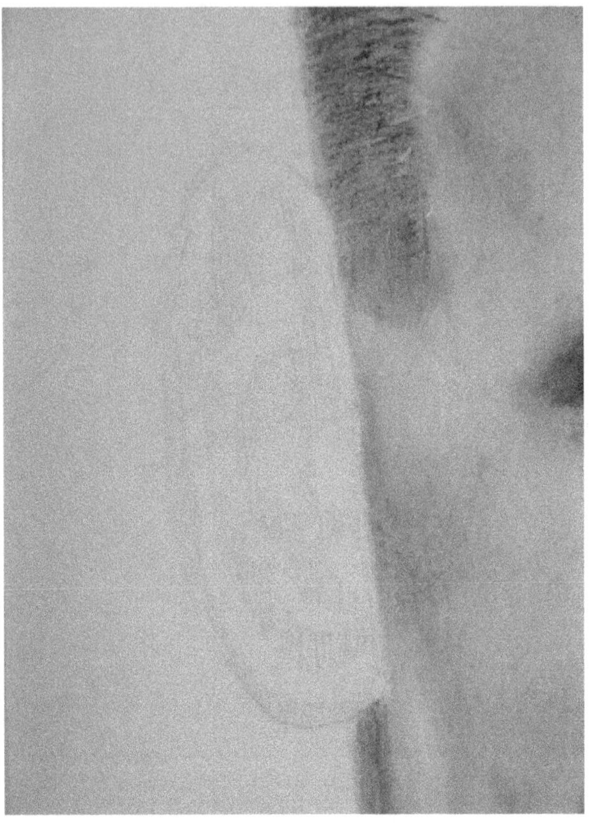

I used a carbon pencil, pressing hard on a piece of scrap paper to make some dust that could be picked up with a paintbrush.

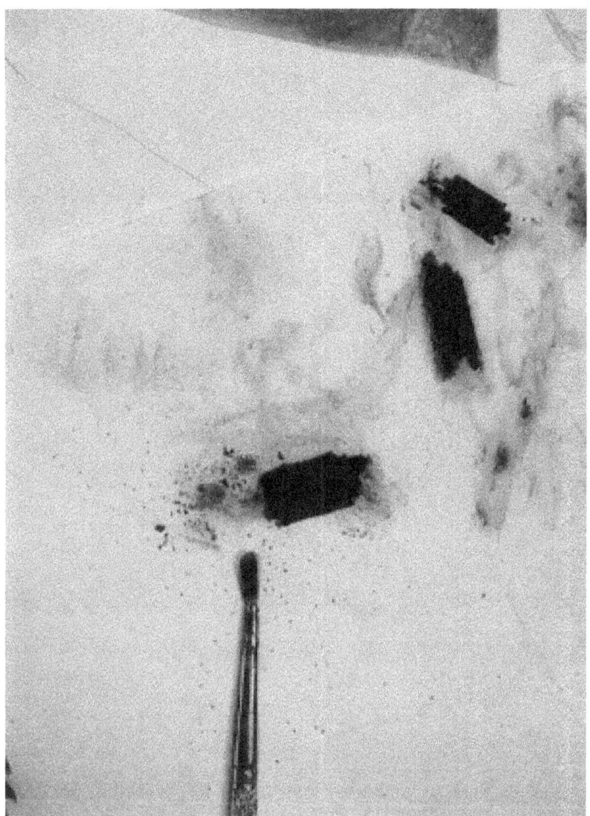

This was painted into the spaces between the highlights that were picked out earlier. Using a paintbrush avoids hard edges and additionally, the ear is not a focal point of the composition, so to keep it out of focus and soft assists the entire portrait with realism and the 3D effect.

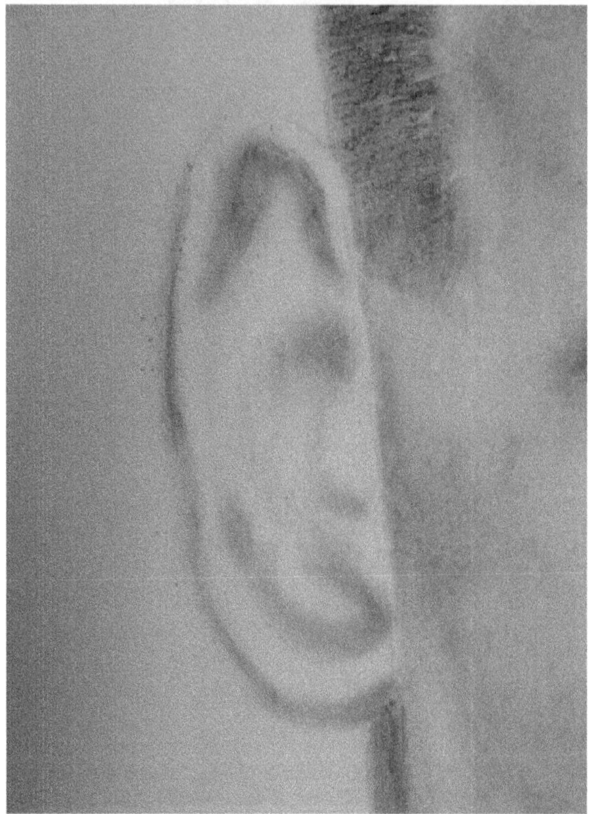

Now it's time for punching-up. (Make the darkest values as deep as needed).

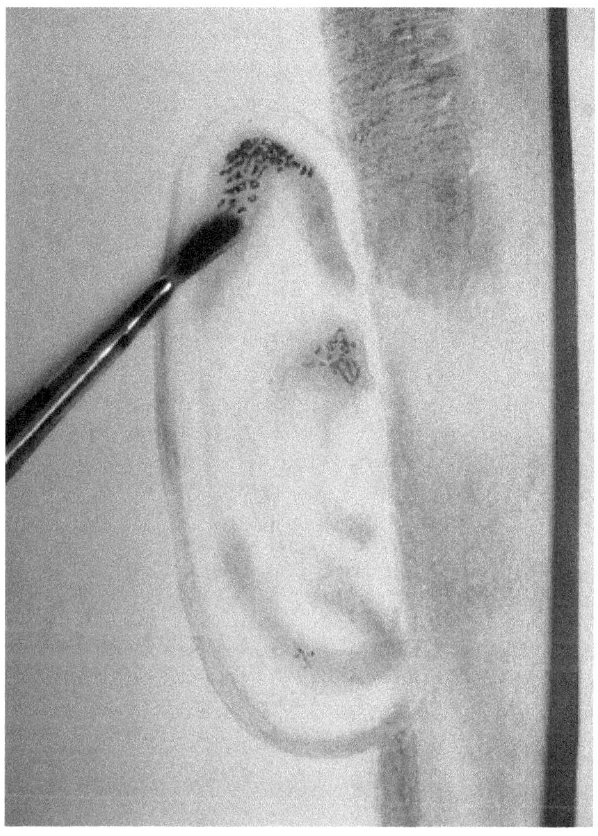

Since the light comes from above, the darkest shadow is below the fold at the top.

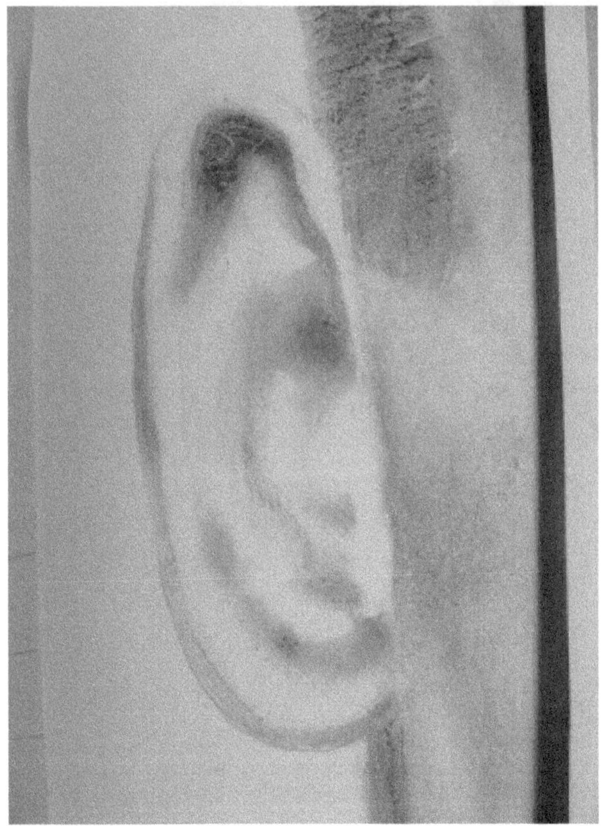

The final stage is to use a hard pencil and lay down circularism layers to depict the rolling form of the folds in the ear. This stage is to adjust the transition from dark to light. You might need to use a few grades of pencil to get the subtle shading right.

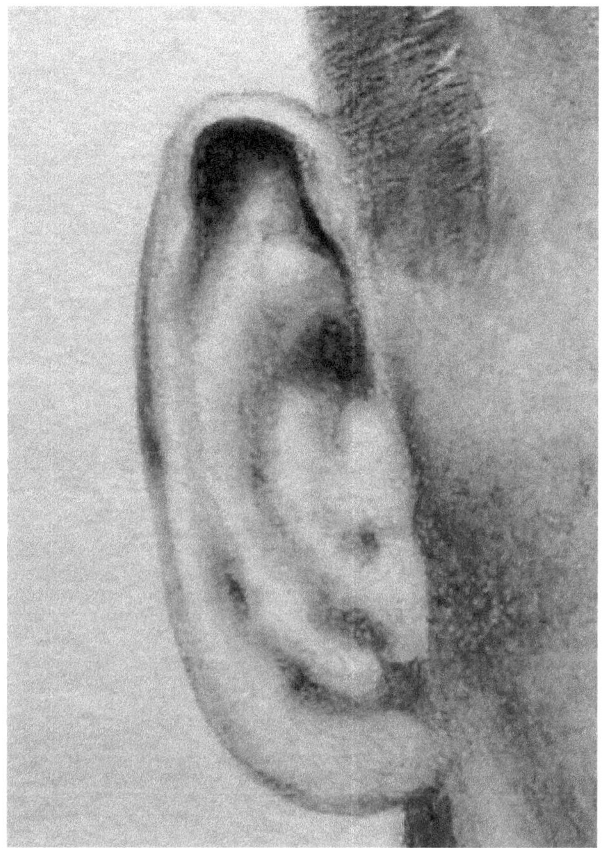

Here is the rest of the portrait to put it in context.

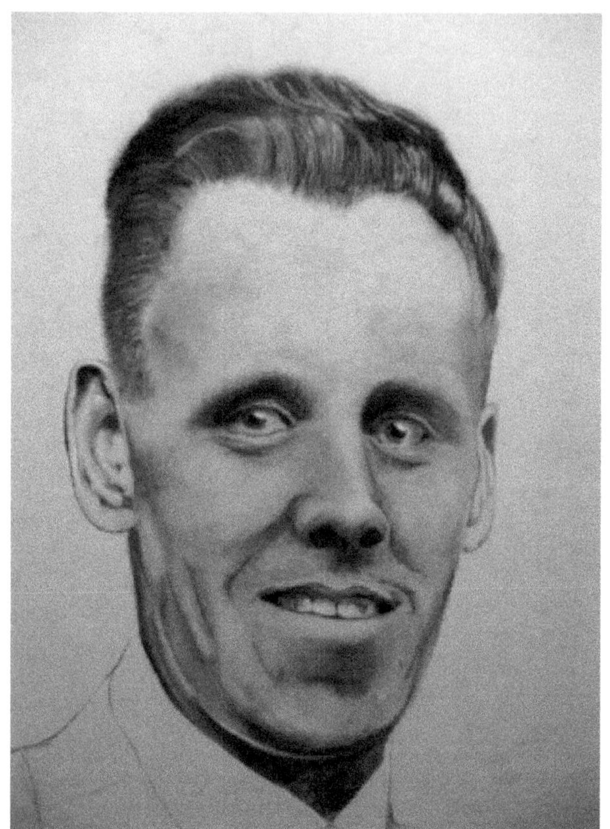

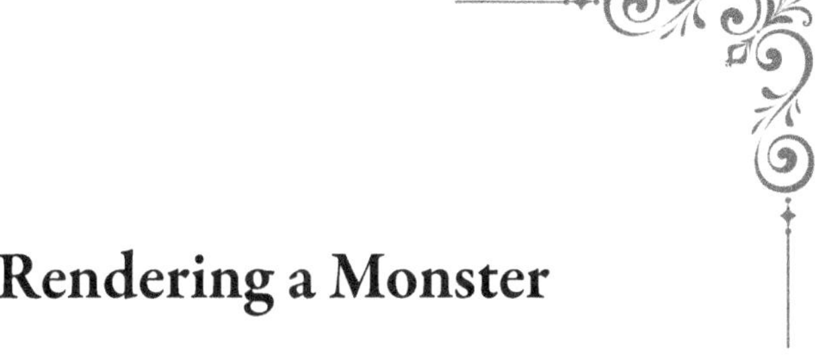

Rendering a Monster

I've read that many people who would like to draw portraits have a go, find that it's too difficult then give up. This is a shame, so I'd like to change that. I've found there is much that often goes wrong when drawing a portrait. Some features of the human face are incredibly sensitive to tiny errors in proportion. Even a dot in the wrong place or a transition that is off by a millimetre can sometimes dramatically alter the result.

I'd like to introduce an element of portrait drawing where you can ignore these issues legitimately. It involves rendering a drawing done by a child. Get a kid to draw a monster's face using contour lines, and render it using the rules below. For a monster, there are no particular requirements for perfect proportion or beauty. That's great because we can concentrate on rendering.

I've also noticed that a lot of portraits might have good proportion, but the artist does not control the lighting properly. The control of lighting is a primary concern of rendering and this means something specific in the context of drawing. Unfortunately, a solid definition that fits this context seems difficult to unearth. At one extreme the word means to extract lard from animal fat. Clearly that's not what we need. Another means to express an idea through artistic representation. That might be true too but it's not specific enough.

For us, rendering means to depict on a flat surface: the form, light, shadow and texture of a three-dimensional object. To do this, you need to copy roughly what a computer-graphics engine does when a two-dimensional model is computed into a 3D model with a particular light source and viewpoint.

Imagine a ray of light from the light source and follow a few basic rules to arrive at a chosen value for the objects where the light ray hits. This sounds complicated but it's really easy.

To develop these rules, let's assume that you are looking at a plane object like a sign. The source of light comes from a strong headlamp mounted on your helmet.

Flat Objects

Rule 1: The sign will be brightest when it is exactly perpendicular to your viewpoint. This means that the sign is front-on. The rays of light come from the headlamp, hit the sign and bounce back into your eye.

Rule 2: How much light that comes back depends on the texture of the surface. If that top sign was covered by a rough cloth, it would not be as bright because the light that hits the sign is scattered in many directions. Only a few light rays come directly back to your eye.

Rule 3: How much light you get back depends on how reflective is the surface. If that sign was a mirror, you would be blinded by the returning light. All the light will return to your eye.

Rule 4: How much light that returns to your eye depends on the angle of the sign. Assume you turn it almost edge-on; the surface of the sign still receives the light rays but the only ones that come back to your eye are from tiny little imperfections in the surface. These imperfections (texture) contain smaller surfaces that are perpendicular to your viewpoint. As the sign is rotated back to you, it will gradually get brighter because more texture-surfaces are perpendicular with your viewpoint.

Rule 5: The amount of light that returns depends on the colour of the object. If the object was perfectly black it would return no light from any angle. Certain colours are naturally brighter—like yellow compared with purple. For a comparable chroma, a yellow sign will appear lighter than a purple sign.

Form-objects

A form-object is something with multiple surfaces. Of course, texture is really caused by form-objects on a surface, but we need to treat texture differently because the scale of texture is much smaller than the overall object. A form-object with multiple surfaces is something like a cube or a sphere or a curtain. The cube has distinct large flat surfaces that are joined by edges. The sphere has one curved surface, and a curtain is a collection of curved surfaces joined by edges. You could approximate a sphere using a regular multifaceted solid. Let's pretend there are 10,000 faces on a regular solid. This is not strictly a sphere, but it would surely look like one. With that in mind, if you can render a cube or a sign or a curtain, you can render a sphere. Simply treat every spot on the sphere as a little surface and imagine what angle it is from your viewpoint, and the light source.

For the curtain, the undulating surfaces could be thought of as simpler surfaces joined by transitions. This is the real key to rendering. If you can break down your object under study into a manageable number of surfaces, then join them using transitions, the result will be a convincing 3D representation.

At the same time of course, you need to consider the texture of the surface. For a curtain, the texture is likely to be consistent. But a portrait will contain typically four main textures: skin, hair, clothing and shiny mechanical objects. You should treat each of these textures consistently within their own area, and make them appear to return the right amount of light compared with the other textures.

Rule 6: The amount of light that is received by the object depends not only on the light source, but also on light that is reflected by nearby objects.

Please consider the illustration below.

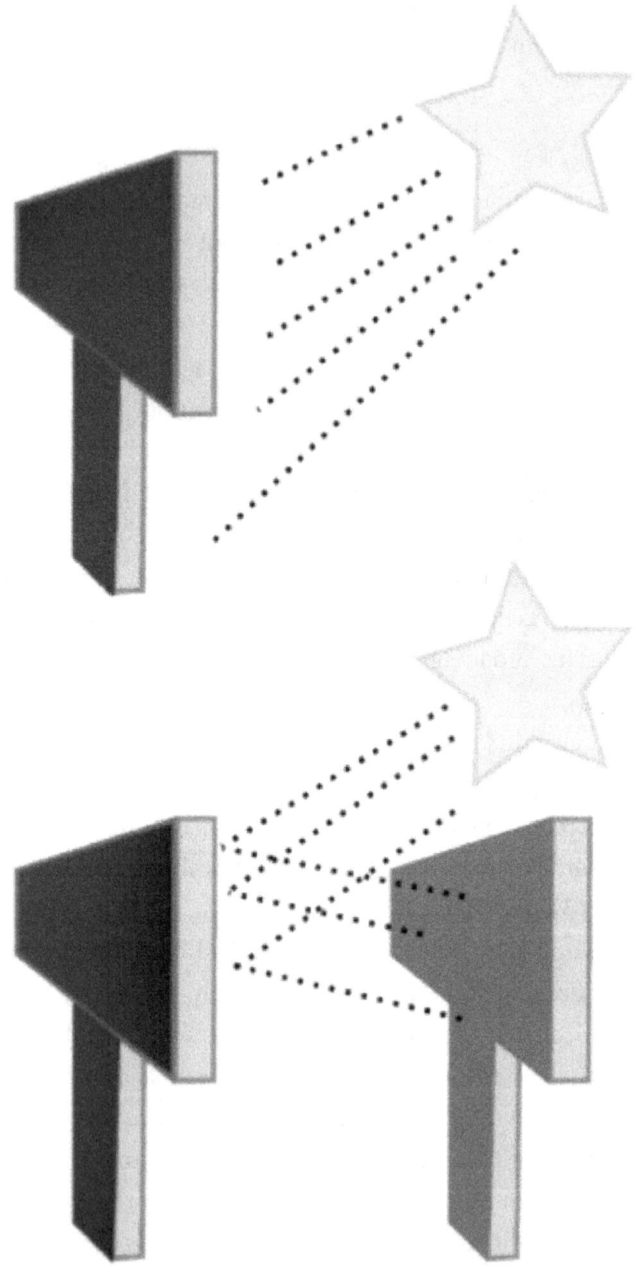

In the top scene, the sign is isolated, and the light source comes from the top right, so the back of the sign will be totally black no matter its colour and texture. The nearby edges will reflect some rays of light into your eye and will have a midvalue.

In the lower situation where there are two signs that are otherwise isolated, the sign most to the left will be like the one above, but the one to the right of it will receive some reflected light off the hidden surface of the one to its left.

Here is a child's drawing of a monster's head, and a rendered copy. It's a good example because there are several distinct surfaces presented at different angles to the viewer. The eyes have a different texture. I've assumed the light comes from the top right.

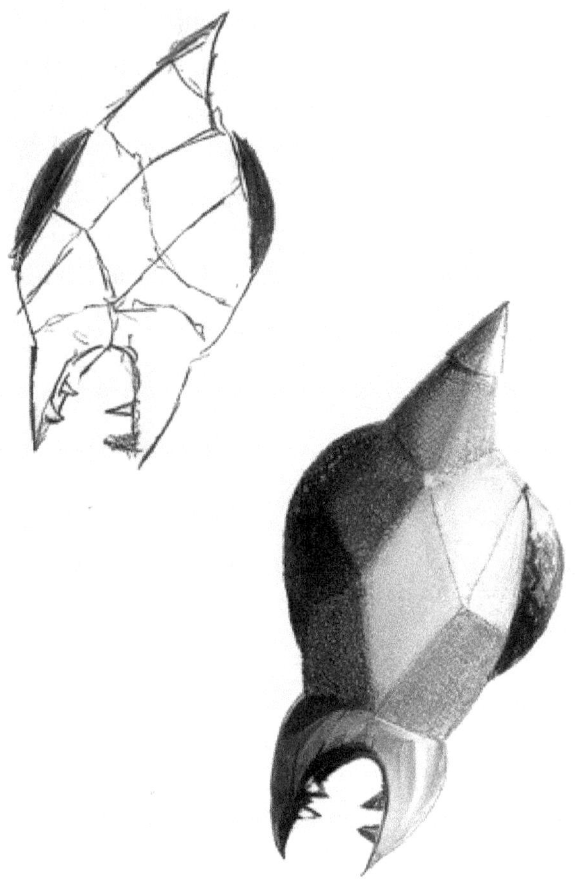

Kids have great ideas! More on Strategic lines.

Sometimes you have to work from a photograph as in this posthumous portrait. One way to approach a study like this is to pick out angles and key features. By using these lines you will get a feel for proportion and how one element is linked to another.

If I were to use this method, I would scan the photograph into a computer, and print it out in black-and-white. Then take a ruler and draw lines along major angles—like the angle of the mouth, and along the jaw line. Draw one along the nose and two that enclose the eyes. There are no particular rules for this exercise. You just need to choose key features and make note of how they join.

As you get more experienced with this method, you will gradually use fewer lines. Eventually, it will be possible to imagine these lines on your drawing surface. There is no harm in actually drawing them though. Initially, use a ruler and measure them exactly to the millimetre.

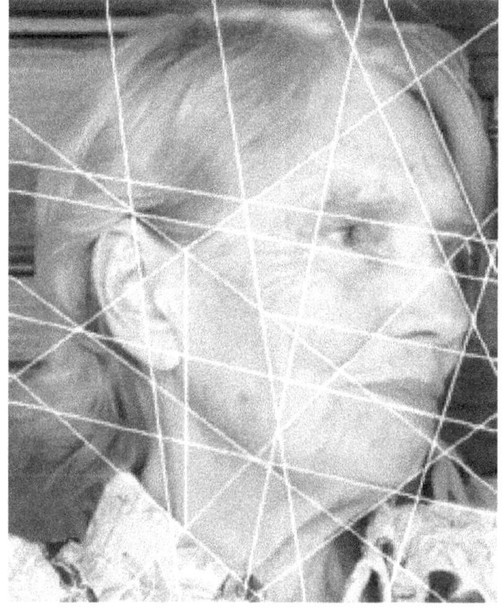

Draw these lines on your paper. Use a very light touch and a sharp HB pencil.

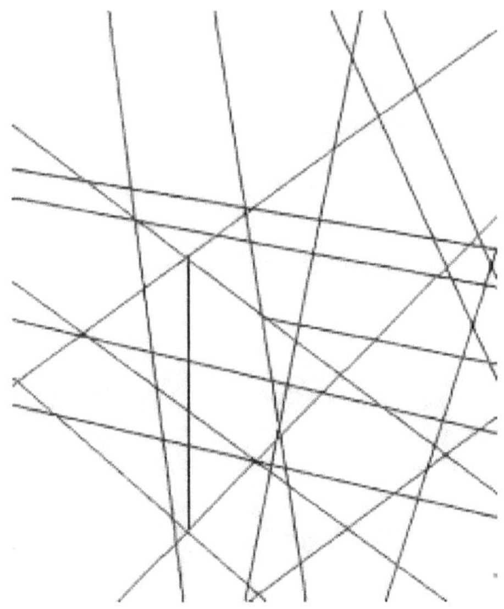

Now you can start with some contours and identification of transitions.

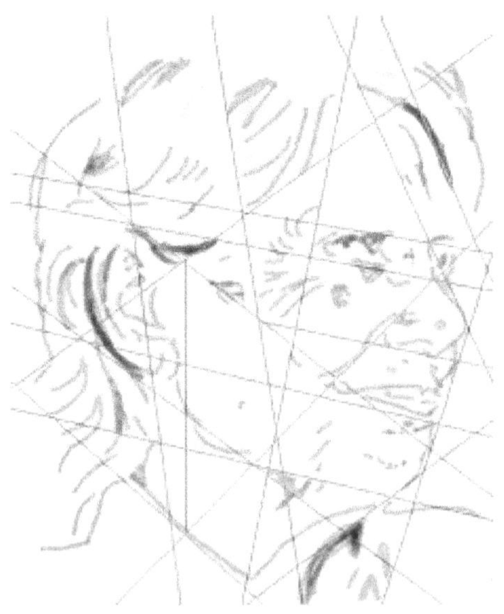

There are a few things to note at this stage. Firstly, the eyes are almost abstract. It's only the context that makes them look like eyes. If you try to draw what you know about eyes at this stage, it will look very odd and false. You need to concentrate on transitions and on surfaces as described above in the section on rendering. These strategic lines and some of the contour lines will be erased as we render the portrait. Some of the lines and contours will be light enough to disappear as you start rendering.

You may begin with any feature, but it's a good idea to decide on the background now and put that in because of the effect of simultaneous contrast. If you want a dark background, render that now. This will make it easier to judge the values as you progress. Then look for dark areas that you are confident about. In this example, the dark areas are the pupils, behind the ears, and part of the clothing under the chin.

The light source in this picture is coming from behind the viewer. You can tell this from the highlight on her nose. But there is also ambient light that mutes shadows. You can deduce this because of the highlight in her eyes. There are two highlights in her right eye where the one on our left is from a light source behind us.

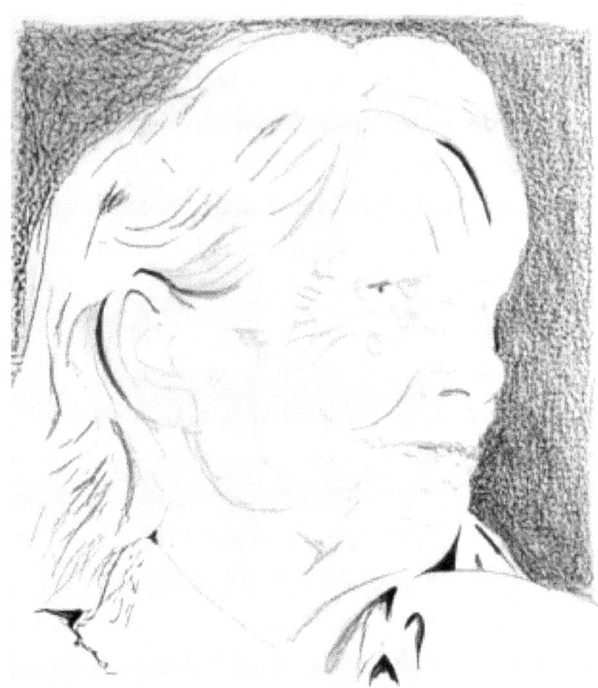

This is the time to start squinting at your drawing, and at the reference to compare values. We are not concerned about detail or texture at this point. The idea is to develop the overall tones. I've started with a carbon pencil with a smooth wedge tip. Rotate the smooth wedge onto its side when needed to create the more defined dark areas. This stage is impressionistic. Now change to a soft graphite pencil and put in some of the darker skin tones. Use a light crosshatch with a smooth round tip. Do not crush the tooth. Blend the darks in the background using a small paintbrush. Use the paintbrush on the darker skin tones to obscure some of the crosshatch.

You can pick up dust from the background to transfer to darker skin. Be careful with this carbon dust because it's difficult to remove. Don't put any on the lighter tones. Put some dust into the darker shadows in the hair.

Most paintings and drawings go through what the artist calls "the ugly stage". This is not to be derogatory about the subject. It means the values placed so far don't agree with the rest of the drawing. It's an in-between stage that most artists feel uncertain and uncomfortable with. The next progress picture is approaching this stage. Some of the darks are in place, but none of the midvalue—and the hair is clearly off-putting. Nevertheless, we need to push on past this stage.

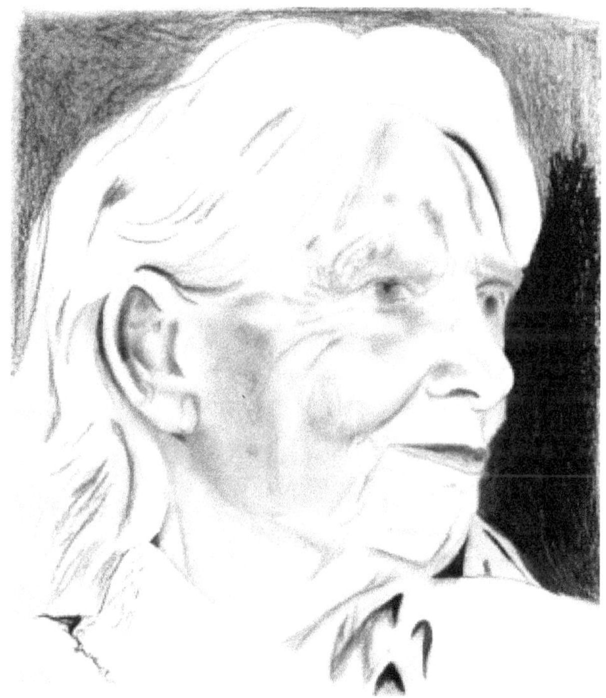

Of course, the background is not complete, but there is enough there to help judge the values for the rest of the drawing.

This is when to really start checking for proper proportion. One great trick is to view the image small—like postage stamp size, and to look at it in a mirror and upside-down. You also need to let your eye take a rest from the image for a while. Stop work, do something else, then come back to it. For some reason, your eye-brain system can get overloaded and trick you into seeing what you think you should see, and not what is actually there. This can work both ways too. I once had a drawing that I thought was so terrible that I would not show it to anyone. I was really unhappy with it and put it away for almost a year. When I got it out again, it looked fine! Many portrait artists will tell you stories like this.

When you are drawing with the carbon pencil, it makes some dust and it's really tempting to blow it away. This is sometimes not a good idea because after a long period of concentration, you might have built up excess saliva. Blowing some of that across your work is a little upsetting. (Yes. This really happens.) Pick up the paper, tip it to one side and use a blower-brush as sold for cleaning camera lenses. Or simply be mindful of this potential problem and blow clean air.

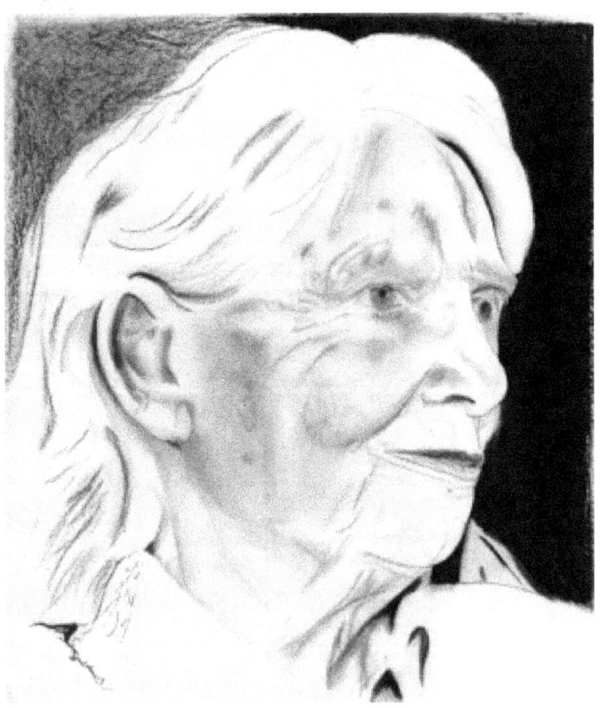

At this stage, you can see how important high contrast is for a dramatic image. The actual portrait has mostly midvalues because this lady has light-coloured hair and skin colours, also because of the scattered ambient lighting, there are few dark shadows within the face. I have deliberately deepened the shadows in her ear, behind the ear, and under the chin. This helps to hold it all together visually, and will also provide a value-anchor for the rest of the skin tones. When we start rendering, to have deep darks nearby allows us to add more texture but still keep a luminous effect. If these darks were absent, the skin would look too dark.

In the above picture, you should be able to see that I made a proportion adjustment around her chin. It's now apparent there are two main features of this portrait that need to stand out. The creases around her eyes strongly suggest the lady smiled easily and often. We need to retain this effect. Her mouth seems to be closed consciously, and that is probably because she did not want to show her teeth. I have many other photographs and visual memory to confirm this. Despite the closed lips, there is a hint of a calm relaxed smile. I want to maintain a state of calmness and acceptance in the somewhat distant gaze, because this lady was suffering from terminal cancer at the time and only had weeks left to live.

I am now carefully comparing all the features one by one. The best way to do this is to isolate a small area of the reference using a viewing hole as described earlier in the subsection called *Locate abstract shapes.*

At this stage, I can see some adjustments are required in the detail of the ear, her right upper eyelid, a little bit of her left upper eyelid, some shadows on the cheek, and a few adjustments around her neck. I've marked these on the picture below. Where there are little crosses, it means to erase or mute the value. It's these minor changes that make the difference between a portrait that is comfortable to view compared with one that feels 'wrong'.

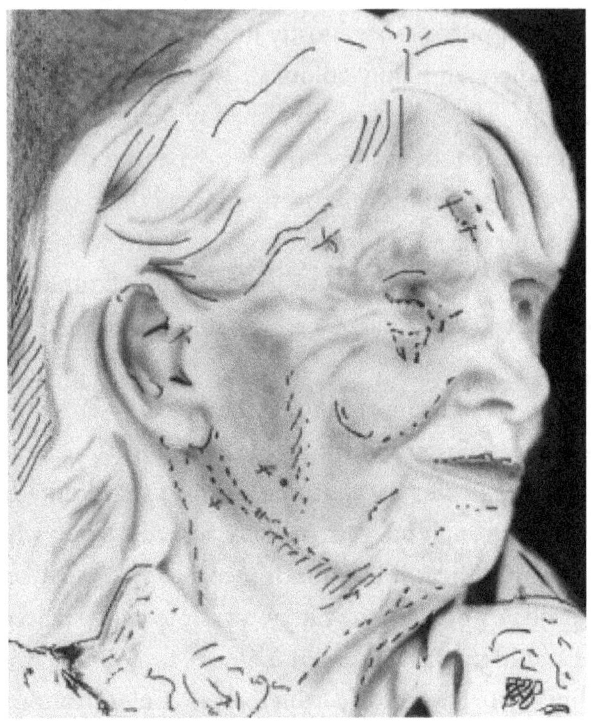

Here it is after making some of these adjustments:

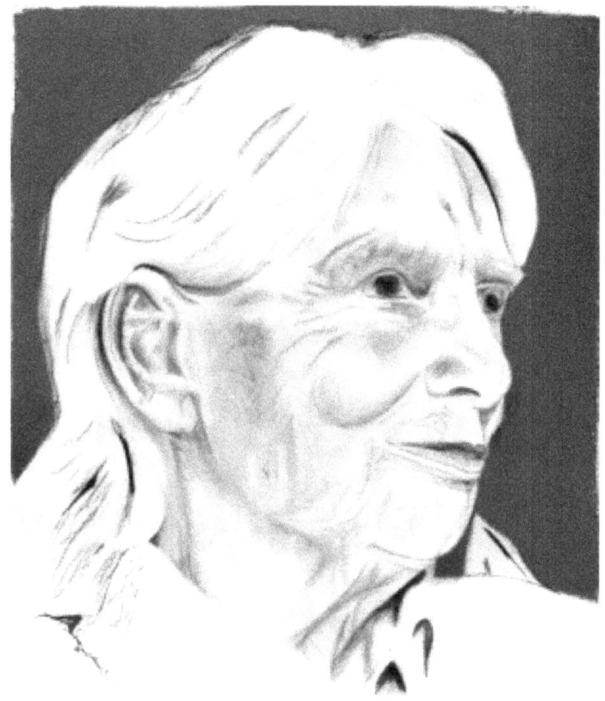

There are still some worries but nothing serious. Her cheek is a little overstated but that will become less of a problem after putting down the texture and unifying the values. The sunburnt look is caused by simultaneous contrast with her unrendered hair. The large area of white forces you to see the values in her face darker than they will be when the hair has been rendered.

One way to tackle hair like this is to brush in a layer of graphite dust then pick out highlights. We have already put some of the shadows in and these serve as guides for the way the layers of hair fall. Later, some texture will be added. Note that I pulled in some of the background carbon into the edges of the hair. This is because there is no well-defined edge, and doing this blurs that transition. It obscures lines that were present before using the brush. Hair that is thin and light will be wispy which will allow some light to pass through it. We expect to see some of the background around the edges. We want the viewer to focus on the eyes, nose and mouth in this portrait and the hair does not need to be highly focused.

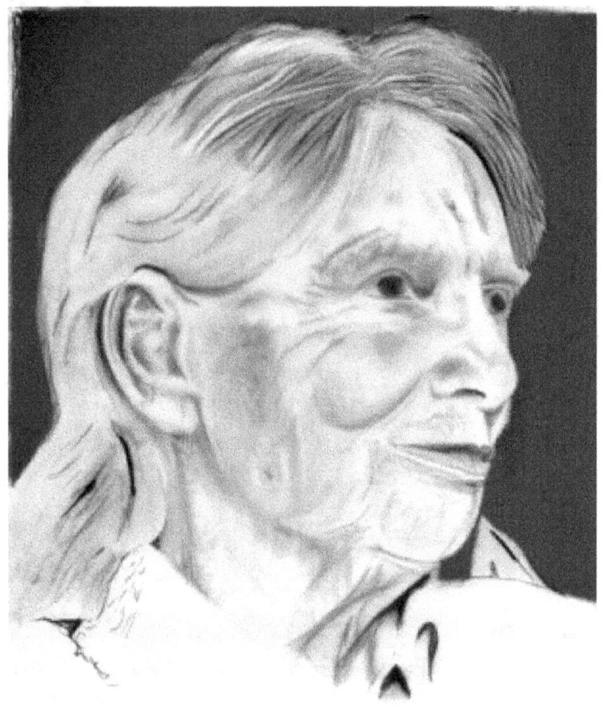

Above, you can see that I've started to lay down texture in her hair. This is done with a sharp 4H mechanical pencil, followed by a sharp 2B mechanical pencil. The highlights were first picked out with an eraser, which was easy to do because graphite dust that has been applied with a soft brush does not stick hard in the tooth. The general idea is to use relatively short strokes, close together to arrive at texture but not detail. Follow the curves of the hair and upgrade shadows here and there as it seems appropriate. When all the hair has been done, I'll blend some of it with a tortillon to further mute the pencil strokes.

The next stage is to start rendering the mid values of the skin tones and put in detail of skin texture. Render small bumps, freckles, dips and creases by using a combination of HB and 4H circularism, smudging with a dirty tortillon. Pay close attention to the eyes. Be sure to render each as a sphere, which requires shading in the corners. Pull out the highlights in the eye using the kneadable eraser by moulding it into a point and repeatedly gently dragging it across the highlight. Re-mold the eraser and repeat this process until you get the desired effect. Eyebrows and eyelashes are only subtly suggested—especially for an older lady who is not using mascara. In this case, her eyelashes are blond and are hardly visible. If you try to put eyelashes and eyebrows in strongly to a drawing like this it will look false.

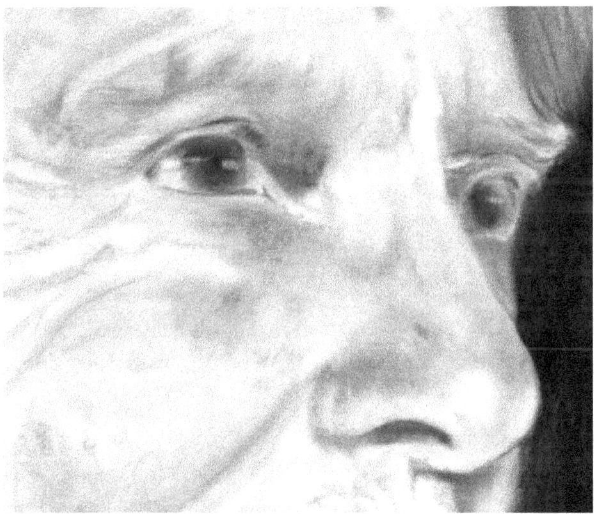

The shadows under and to the left of the nose are important for a 3D effect. There are two highlights on the nose as there are in the eyes. In her cheek, I used a few layers as follows: 4H circularism followed by some 2B circularism, then dabs with the eraser and 4H circularism again. This gives that look where the skin is slightly dimpled as if it is faceted. When you do the circularism, hold the pencil right at the end and don't press. Just let the weight of the pencil make the mark. You will not be able to see each individual mark—or at least will barely be able to see it, but as you do many more circles, the change in value will be apparent. The texture will appear eventually.

This is the final illustration. As always, I don't know if it is finished. Many artists keep finding little things to adjust or enhance but at some point, like this book, you need to declare it complete.

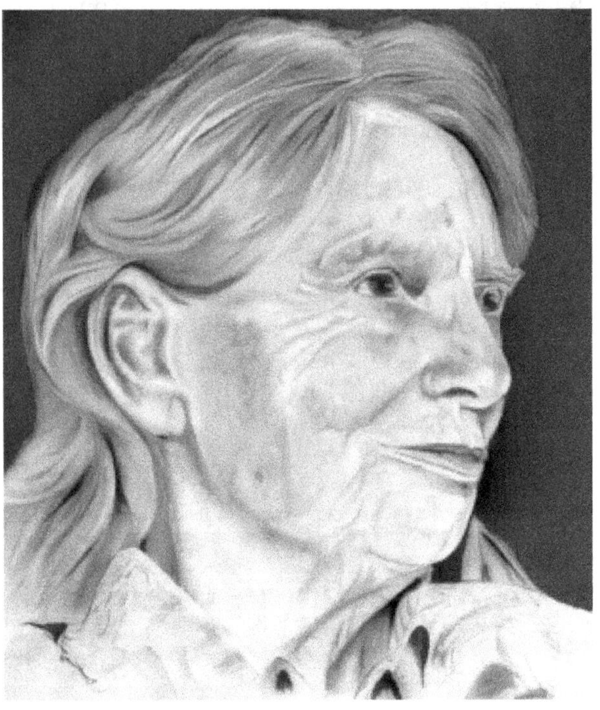

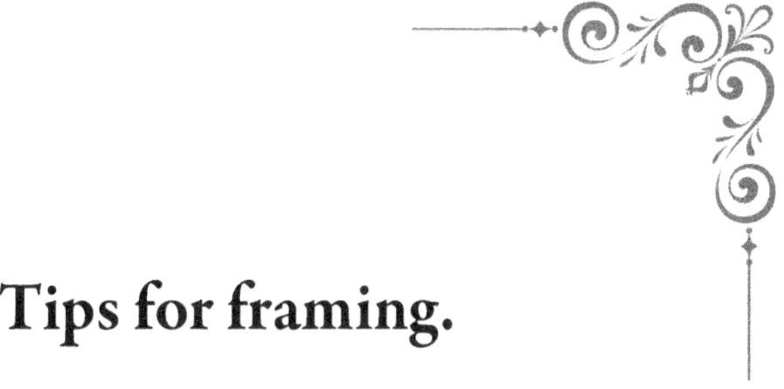

Tips for framing.

Graphite is attracted to electrically charged surfaces. It's the same mechanism that causes your hair to stand on end when near a balloon that's been electrically charged. Plastic can often gain static electricity and this means you should not use Poly(methyl methacrylate) (PMMA), also known as acrylic glass, and by the brand names Lucite and Perspex. You should not store the drawings in a plastic sleeve for the same reason. Over time, the charged surface will lift some of the graphite off the paper.

Instead, use picture glass, or preferably museum quality glass. The latter will stop 95% of ultraviolet rays. This is important over the long term because the UV light is involved with yellowing of the paper. Museum glass is expensive but antireflective. Normal picture glass will limit your viewing pleasure because of numerous reflections.

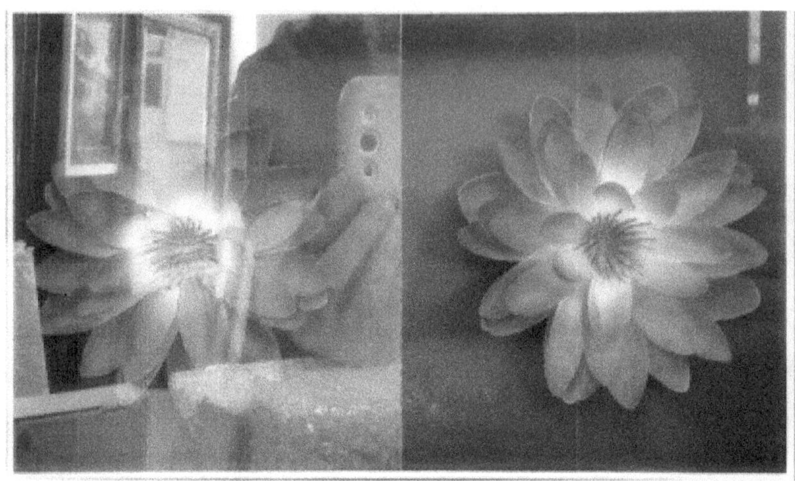

When you use glass in a frame, also use a mount because it will separate the glass from the picture and allow any loose particles to drop out of sight.

Den glass is a cheaper antireflective option but will not block UV.

Graphite, charcoal and carbon are chemically stable even in the presence of UV, but if left unprotected will wear away mechanically. If you decide not to use glass, it's best to spray the work with a fixative. Note that doing this slightly darkens the drawing. Some people use hair spray but I am suspicious of the archival properties of hair spray because there might be unnecessary chemicals in it.

Often, a plain matte or gloss black frame is best for graphite artwork. To use colour is likely to detract from the drawing. A slightly cream coloured mat board works well too because the off-white tint can help to enhance the highlights.

Place small rubber pads on the back lower corners to help prevent the picture from tilting. Another trick is to put a single loop in the hanging string over the nail because that stops the string sliding.

The string on the back of the frame is attached on each side by picture rings. Place these near the top to make the picture stand flat against the wall, and lower to make it drop forward. Letting it drop forward might help to prevent reflections.

Another great tip is to first find a frame, then obtain the paper and construct your composition to work within the mat board area. In this way, you are purchasing stock-frames and making the picture fit rather than the more expensive alternative where you need a custom frame.

Here are some "rules of thumb"

· Use a simple frame if your composition is detailed or complex.

· Use an ornate frame for simple subjects.

· If your light source in the drawing appears to come from the top right, try to hang it in a room where the actual light also comes from the top right.

· Use a slightly wider margin at the base of the mat board. This helps to anchor the picture visually.

· When you attach the drawing to the back of the mat board, use only one piece of non-yellowing high-quality tape. This is typically sold for book-repair. Put this tape along the top of the back of the picture to attach it to the mat board. In this way, as moisture slightly alters the dimensions of the paper, it will not buckle.

Thank you

Good luck with your drawing. I once said that a work of art is the result of a series of mistakes. Although that's meant as a joke, in some ways it is true. Don't worry if your initial efforts are unpleasant. Don't worry if your 100th effort has issues. The main aim is to improve your powers of observation and technique. Skills learned with the pencil will translate nicely to skills in other mediums.

Thank you to my friends who read the draft and made many suggestions.

Don't miss out!

Visit the website below and you can sign up to receive emails whenever Jeremy Lee publishes a new book. There's no charge and no obligation.

https://books2read.com/r/B-A-CAQFB-INCAD

BOOKS 2 READ

Connecting independent readers to independent writers.

Did you love *How to Draw Portraits*? Then you should read *It's About Time*[1] by Jeremy Lee!

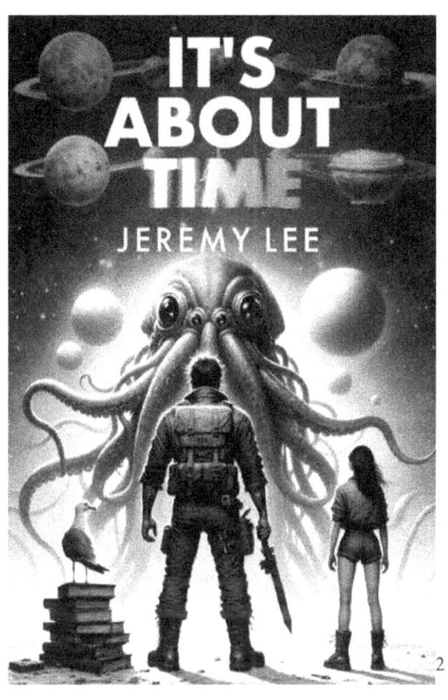

Immerse yourself in 'It's About Time,' the epic tale that touches the boundary of imagination. Meet Og, alias Darg, an immortal caught in the web of alien scientists that reshape the fabric of existence. As he ventures through a besieged universe, Og's path is one of profound metamorphosis—from an existence as a machine to the complexities of human emotion, including the most transformative of all: love. Alongside a fiery young woman and a steadfast elder, he stands against a dark force holding Earth in its grip. This story masterfully intertwines a diverse cast, each with unique powers and ambitions, against a backdrop of suspense, scientific intrigue, and the timeless search for connection. With every twist, 'It's About Time' challenges the

---

1. https://books2read.com/u/4jYlql

2. https://books2read.com/u/4jYlql

boundaries between human and machine, incredible terrifying isolation and companionship, despair and hope. For anyone who delights in unraveling the mysteries of the cosmos and the heart, this journey is yours to explore. Offering more than just a narrative, it invites readers into a universe where the impossible becomes possible, where love defies logic, and where a long term hermit must become a leader to save his world. Prepare for an adventure where emotion and intellect collide, making 'It's About Time' a must-read for enthusiasts and novices of science fiction alike.

Read more at https://guardiancybertech.com.au/books.

Also by Jeremy Lee

How to Draw Portraits
It's About Time

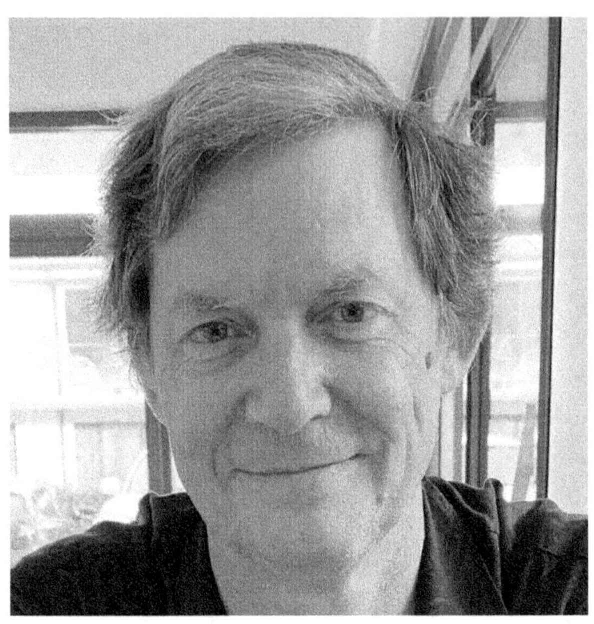

About the Author

Jeremy Lee is a Canadian by birth, currently living in Australia. He has been drawing and painting for as long as he can remember. Jeremy grew up in various parts of England including the picturesque Cotswolds. He picked up a camera before the age of ten, and distinctly remembers starting his first significant artwork at the age of six. Fascinated by colour, Jeremy spent many long nights and evenings learning the physics. It seems easy at first to explain why something is 'red' or 'green' but the more you look into it, the more difficult it becomes. As it happens, the study of colour leads you deep into quantum physics. This created an interest in electronics and he built an electronic organ at age 14. Around the same age, he sold many picture-sculptures to friends and family. When older, he created glass engravings and distributed them as wedding presents and sold them. He worked for several years as an assistant at Winchcombe Pottery, run by Ray Finch. At the end of his tenure, Ray offered Jeremy an apprenticeship. At a crossroads in life, with opportunities as a full time potter or to pursue the Olympics as a gymnast, Jeremy decided that a long term career would be best served pursuing his love of science. Jeremy now has a degree in electronics, and is a certified internet security professional. This is what pays the bills and looks after his dependents and a large pole house that he built as an owner-builder; but his wife, children, then art and craft and working with wood takes the most prominent place in his life. While in his early teens, he was disqualified from a local art and craft competition for 'cheating'. This, being a mystery and great source of irritation caused his parents to try and find out why and it turns out that the judges truly believed that the work was pre-bought and not constructed by a young man. Jeremy considered this a lesson in life, but is yet to work out what it is. In 1988, a painting of Jeremy's on display at a local shop was stolen. On the one hand, he considers that something of a back-handed compliment but on the other wonders why the customer felt that it was worth stealing but not paying for.

Read more at https://guardiancybertech.com.au/books.

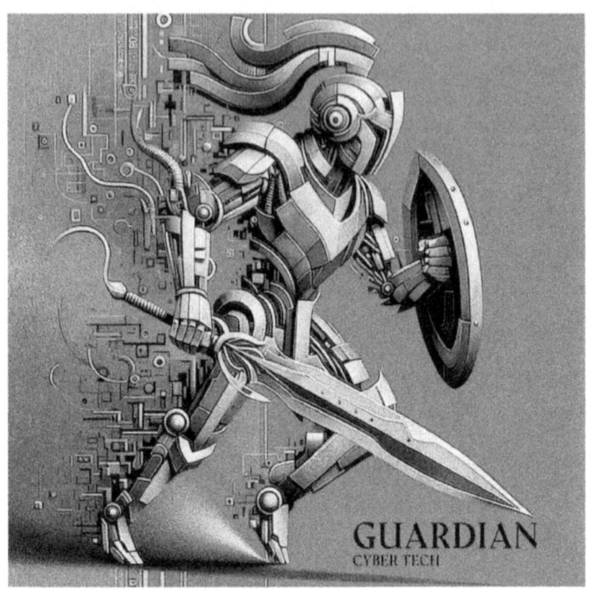

About the Publisher

Guardian Cyber Tech specialises in computer security services and educational material. The book division publishes non-computer related educational material and novels. GCT is Australian owned.

Read more at https://GuardianCyberTech.com.au/books.